Communicating with
the Fourth Dimension

ISBN 978-1-62141-233-5

Published 2012 by AstroProjections, 10090 Kern River Court, Rancho Cordova, California, 95670 U.S.A. All rights reserved. No part of this publication may be reproduced, stored in a retrieval system, or transmitted in any form or by any means, electronic, mechanical, recording or otherwise, without the prior written permission of the author, available at http://www.janicestork.com.

Printed in the United States of America.

BookLocker.com, Inc.
2012

Cover design by Todd Engel

FREE interview with the author, and pictures from the book, are available online at www.janicestork.com. The YouTube video that contains the interview and pictures was created and directed by Dianna Wareing.

Communicating with the Fourth Dimension

Janice A. Stork

"We do not see things as they are.
We see things as we are."
--Talmud--

Acknowledgments

Thanks to my sons, William and Jon, for supporting me while writing this book and to all my friends who became a part of it since I started this journey.

Special thanks to JoAnn Lara and Linda Beauregard-Vasquez for their input on content and for their longtime friendship as well.

Heartfelt thanks goes to Akar, my Spirit guide who was always by my side when I ventured off into another dimension.

Prologue

I could feel the chilling breath of the morning breeze embracing my body as I stood listening to small waves crashing on the river rocks beneath my feet. My eyes followed the rocks into the crystal clear water until they disappeared into the darkness. It was in that darkness that I often found a fish swimming. I never knew if it would be a small fish, or if I were lucky maybe a school of them. The place was the American River which is upstream from the Sacramento River. The Sacramento River was named after the California town where I live and is known for its salmon. Above the water, I could see a flock of ducks riding the waves. The sun, glistening on the rapidly moving water, kissed me on the cheek before disappearing behind the morning mist.

My hand felt a quick jerk from the blue leash it was holding. "What is it, Max?" I asked, looking down at my white dog with his fluffy long tail; he was eagerly sniffing the scent of a man or animal he wanted to track. I pulled him back towards me before he sent both of us tumbling into the water.

Everybody who knows me knows I am not a dog person. My heart belongs to two cats. Kiera is my black cat that I call my "slut" because she is streetwise. She delights in sitting outside on a brick ledge that is the back of my fireplace. From there, she watches people passing my hedge without them being able to see her. She's also my mouser. I counted 13 mice she killed within two weeks in the spring. She never gets sick. In contrast, the real love of my life is Simba. He is an orange and white cat with fur like a rabbit and is so gorgeous he isn't allowed outside my fenced yard like Kiera. Fortunately for me, he tops the scales at 22 pounds and couldn't jump on a fence if he had to do so. Simba is Max's best friend, and they love to play on the floor with each other. It was hard in the beginning to train them not to bite when they played. A cat's bite is extremely toxic and could kill an animal and probably a person if the wound gets infected; whereas, a dog's bite isn't toxic unless they have rabies or some other disease.

The fact that I had never been a dog person made the way Max entered my life even more surreal. One day, I had a vision of a dog I would someday own. It happened the same way as it did when I had a vision of the home that I now actually do own. I bought my home two years ago, and it all happened just like I had seen in the vision. I was told about the handyman who would help me, about the location of the parking, about the shade trees in the back yard, and about the fact that it would be within walking distance to the river.

At the time I had the vision of the dog, I didn't know I would own him. In my mind's eye, there was a white fluffy dog that wasn't very big. I remember it was the day after Thanksgiving. People were visiting relatives or recouping from family gatherings when I found myself scanning through Craigslist, a website that contains classified ads where people can buy and sell things. This particular day, I stumbled into the pet section, and there was Maximus. The ad described him as a Maltese-Poodle that loved children. I immediately called the owner who lived about an hour from my home and then drove out to get him. A few weeks would pass before I would realize that I had bought the exact same dog as the one I had in my vision. I purchased him for one hundred and twenty five dollars. Later, I learned from a vet who fell in love with Max that his breed would normally cost several hundred dollars more. Kismet, timing, looking for a dog when others were still celebrating the holidays -- those things were the mixture it took, and when the moment appeared, I jumped and captured the dog the Universe wanted me to have.

Max pulled hard on his leash as he sniffed the ground. Then, his tale started wagging. "Ruff, Ruff," he barked. "Ruff, Ruff, Ruff."

"You silly dog," I smiled, adding, "That is not one of Mama's turtles. That is a river turtle. This is his home." Max tilted his head back and forth as he studied my words and looked back at the turtle as he wagged his tail with excitement. I reached down to pat him on his head as I nudged his collar away from the turtle. He thought he was doing what he does at home when he helps me find one of my box turtles that are hiding from me in my back yard.

I didn't use to be a turtle person either. Turtles heads look like snakes, and I am DEATHLY afraid of snakes. One morning, I had just finished cleaning my home when I noticed a small clump of something on the wood floor of my dimly lit hall. Max was housebroken, and the cats buried their droppings in the cat box, so I couldn't figure out what I was looking at or how it ended up on my freshly mopped floor. I raced off to the garage to get a dust pan to pick the clump up. There in the dust pan was a baby turtle with two tiny puncture marks on the back of its shell; he was no larger than a quarter. Right away, I knew that baby turtle was something my black cat Kiera had brought into the house to show me.

Recalling it now, I remember I wasn't so calm. I was panic-stricken. Not knowing what to do, I raced through the garage into the front yard, thinking, "Okay, God, Great Spirit, Universe -- what am I supposed to do now?" Since I was new to the neighborhood, I didn't know any of my neighbors. No sooner had I asked Spirit for help, when suddenly I noticed a young woman who was standing across the street and wondering what all the commotion was about.

"Do you live there?" I urgently asked.

"No, I am here with my husband visiting my mom," the long- haired brunette replied. "What seems to be the matter?"

"My cat brought this turtle into my home, and I don't know what to do with it. I can't just throw it away. It has two small bite marks on it, and it is scared." No doubt I was freaking the poor little creature out doing my panic dance.

"Let me see," she called, walking towards me.

I held out the dust pan for her to look.

"It just so happens that my husband and I are very much into animal husbandry. You could give me the turtle if you like. My mother is taking penicillin for pneumonia. My husband and I can use it to treat the turtle's bites."

"Yes, please take it," I said, watching her hand gently pick up the small wonder.

She walked away excited about the turtle she would be taking back home with her. Later that day, her mother came knocking on my door.

"Hi, my name is Jan," said a woman whose nose was bright red; she was clutching a Kleenex in her hand. "I am your neighbor that lives across the street.

"Hi, that will be an easy name for me to remember since my name is Jan," I greeted her.

"You just made my daughter's and her husband's trip out here extra special with the turtle you gave them. They wanted me to ask if they could examine your backyard to see where it hatched."

"Trust me. The backyard has been thoroughly cleaned in the past few days."

"The mother or father must be around somewhere," she said.

I walked her through the house to my backyard and showed her how clean the yard was. As I suspected, we didn't find a single turtle.

A few months later, I noticed a turtle the size of a half grapefruit walking on my concrete patio. Apparently, it had been hibernating out of sight. I named it Gertrude, and to this day I don't know if it is a male or a female.

That's the way my life was all the time. Spirit (God, Divine Mother, Christ, Saints of all religions, Great Spirit, Universe, and any name of an unseen Divine Force) was always showing me magical things like the young woman who was visiting from out of state that just so happened to be into animal husbandry when a baby turtle needed medical attention and a new home.

The sudden yank of the leash in my hand brought my thoughts back to the river. Max wanted to chase a squirrel he spotted at the base of a tree -- a squirrel that was teasing him by waving its furry brown tail in the air. In squirrel talk, I am sure he was saying, "Dumb dog! You ARE ON A LEASH!"

"Come, Max," I commanded. I was leading him towards the Sunrise Bridge that crosses the river."

"Most people don't even know this place exists," I thought to myself as I watched tiny cars darting across the bridge and carrying drivers anxious to get to where they were going.

I pushed aside some tall brush, and I turned a corner that allowed me to get a better view of the rapids beneath the bridge. The water was alive about 30 feet from shore. Something was jumping up and back down again, but it was too far away from me to make out what I was seeing. Still, the energy coming from it was powerful. Max was content to follow along with his nose moving left to right like a blind man's cane as he sniffed the scents. As I walked closer, I could hear the loud sound of splashing water.

"Oh, my!" I thought to myself. What I was seeing made up for the little fish I didn't see in the dark waters when I first started my walk. I counted at least seven sets of huge salmon spawning with their mates. That fertility was the intense energy I was feeling. November was the time of the year when they fought for their lives while creating new lives, salmon children that would one day return long after their parents had died to do the same thing ... create new life in a season that usually spells out death for most creatures.

Cars will still be racing across the bridge with drivers anxious to get to work, so they can make enough money to go on vacation from the "Rat Race" without realizing the wonder and peace of what nature and the river offered only a stone's throw away.

"It wasn't that long ago when I was like the people in those cars," I thought. "But as I now reflect back at my life, I can see how much I have changed since moving to my new home near the river a couple of years ago."

The truth is that I wasn't the same person anymore. Maybe it was my ripening age of sixty-five with another birthday having come and gone just a few days before my river sojourn. Perhaps I was awakening spiritually because of all the time I had been spending at Ananda learning of the teachings of Paramahansa Yogananda. It really didn't matter which of those things were factors.

"The simple truth is that all my life I have been on a spiritual quest, but now I find myself craving even more spiritual food," I thought as I continued to think about my life. I realized that one of the books that really brought about major changes in my life was a 1500 page book called Bhagavad Gita that supposedly was written 6,000 years before the Bible and was interpreted by Paramahansa Yogananda.

"I am changing physically, too," I thought. Not only did my eyes see things clearer now, but my physical appearance was also changing as I took my spiritual quest much deeper. Excess weight was disappearing, and the graying hair around my face contrasted by the rest of my fawn-brown hair made me look softer and a tad bit wiser but certainly a lot calmer.

Suddenly, a familiar voice spoke in my mind as I walked along the river's edge back towards home, studying multi-colored rocks of varying sizes, some displaying ley lines, that glimmered beneath the clear waters.

"Now," it commanded.

It was the voice of Akar (a name I was once given for my Spirit guide but which represents, for me, God, Divine Mother, Christ, Universe, Saints of all Religions, Great Spirit, and any other name of an unseen Divine Force). I knew what he (he/she) wanted me to do. It wasn't the first time he made his presence known in the past few months.

"Can I?" I thought to myself. "Is it possible for me to still have the strength to write another book let alone the wisdom to do what Akar is asking of me? Write another book about things I have been taught to see and hear as I journeyed with Spirit into other dimensions?"

We are all born with spirit guides. I didn't pay any attention to mine until years later when I heard a voice asking me to roll the window down while driving in the rain on my way to work. I tried arguing with my mind, but fearing I would surely go crazy if the mental dialogue didn't stop, I rolled it down. It was then that I was side-swiped by a huge truck. If I hadn't rolled the window down my face would have been badly cut from the broken glass because I was sitting on the driver's side when the truck plunged into me. The accident left me with a whip lash. But more than that, it dropped me down on my knees and made me ask Akar (Spirit), "What is this world about anyway?"

In the Bible, it is written, "Ask and you shall receive." I have since learned that we have to be careful about what we ask for. Immediately after asking my question regarding our world and our purpose in it, Akar enrolled me in "Spirit School." The classes were often life threatening when they involved many unexpected auto accidents with trucks. The tests that followed revealed how well I had learned my lessons and what I experienced while journeying into other dimensions.

"NOW," the voice came again.

I knew what was expected of me. Akar wanted me to write a book about what I have learned now that I am an elder who is preparing my gown for my eventual graduation from "Spirit School."

"Come, Max. It's time for us to go home," I murmured. Max lapped up some water and then picked up his pace as he charged forth up the sandy embankment in front of us.

Chapter 1

I pushed the door open to my office with my knee. My hand grasped several paint brushes and a heavy can of white paint. I tossed a roll of paper towels and some old newspapers onto my maple desk that was already draped to protect it from spills.

When I first moved into my home I painted the walls of the bedroom that I converted into an office a sky blue which seemed appropriate since it would be used for seeing astrology clients. The trim was all white and the doors to the closet that now held supplies were also painted white.

Tantalizing Eastern music played in the background. Music was important because it changed my vibration, much the same as changing the stations on the radio so you could hear a different song. In my case it changed the channel and opened up a portal so I could hear Akar (Spirit, God, Divine Mother, Christ, Saints of all religions, Great Spirit, Universe, and any name of an unseen Divine Force) and follow his (his/her) lead while I painted. The first time I ever heard Akar's voice in my minds ear was prior to a truck hitting my car. The voice firmly said, "Roll your window down."

"No, I answered. It's raining outside," I responded, never reasoning where the dialogue I was answering came from.

"Roll the window down," the voice insisted again.

"That doesn't make any sense," I reasoned while keeping my eye on the road.

"Roll the window down."

"Maybe I can get some fresh air, while getting wet," I laughed to myself.

Then it happened. A truck traveling in the left lane made a right turn into my lane and struck my car. If the window had been up, the glass would have shattered my face.

I ended up with a painful whiplash but I also awoke to the realization that there was something out there looking out for me.

Sometimes, Akar will give me answers to questions, fine-tune past memories so I could have better clarity, or just directs what color paint to put where when I paint.

The music I was listening to softened my mind opening my heart and soul. I learned the importance of music when I started painting murals throughout my home.

In my backyard you could see different murals painted on my back fence which was a sound barrier made from concrete block. Beneath the wall were two rows of dirt with heavy boards holding the dirt in place, giving it the appearance of tiers on a wedding cake. When you stood on the patio you felt like you were looking up a steep hill. To the right was a life sized Tiki that looked scary with pointed teeth and piercing eyes that was painted to serve as a warning to trespassers. They might not want to experience his savage wrath if they tried to do harm. In the middle of the wall were ocean waves at sunset with a mountain in the distance. To the left was a Tiki hut surrounded with exotic flowers. All the murals were painted, almost in a trance state. As long as I was in that state Akar held back my doubting fears that would have talked me out of attempting such an undertaking as to paint three murals on concrete that I could barely reach the tops of with each one being about 10 feet wide.

My mind studied my office walls. All morning I scanned images on the internet hoping to get an idea on what painted clouds looked like. But the pictures I was seeing looked like clouds that were meant for the walls of a child's nursery. Nothing was real enough for me. I knew I needed texture, nothing could be square, clouds were round and fluffy, and they had to have contrasting colors to bring out the white. I knew the rules because I had studied every book on painting I could for several years when I was painting watercolors. The basic rules were the same no matter what media.

I applied some white paint to the wall with my brush. Then I dabbed a torn sponge into some gray paint and followed up with a sponge with white on it over parts of the gray while still allowing some of the blue of the original wall color to come through it. A three dimensional cloud took form and it was so real it looked like I could reach out and touch it. The only problem was now I had about a hundred more to paint. I didn't seem to mind though because once I painted the first one I knew I could do it. One cloud after another took form and each looked different. While listening to the music I was simultaneously listening to Akar talking away like he usually did when I was in such a tranquil state.

Young girls, just becoming teens, were content to look pretty with the hope of catching the eye of a young boy. As they matured their skills at reeling in men would improve until one day they would marry and people from all over the land would come to see their conquest and bring them gifts in celebration on their wedding day. That's how the thinking was during my generation known as the "baby boomers." My mother tried to groom me for that path by fixing up my hair and buying expensive make-up kits and coloring my hair when I was thirteen. However, my quest in life was different. It was a spiritual one that brought with it many questions about my existence and how a noble God I was taught to worship in church delivered to me such a wicked stepfather. One by one the answers to such questions started revealing themselves to me in a book I reached for in my mother's bookshelf. I sat on

3

the floor of her bedroom reading it. The book was called, Astrology for the Millions, by Grant Lewi.

I couldn't put the book down once I started reading it. It boldly claimed that when a person was born planets that were transiting a zodiac belt in the sky mapped out an individual's life. Then I started reading other astrology books that explained how the three wise men in the Bible followed a planetary configuration in the heavens that foretold the birth of a messiah (Christ) and where the birth of this baby would take place.

I couldn't wait to get to school and share what I was learning about astrology before my Jr. High School speech class. The students and my teacher were fascinated as I spoke about different characteristics of the various signs, making sure I included the dates of those signs. This allowed the students to know if I was talking about them if they were born during that time frame. I was so young and naive then. Now, I had become the wise old crone with countless clients and thousands of astrology charts cast under my belt.

The next cloud I painted needed some touch ups to make it look larger than the others. Keeping things different sizes kept a painting interesting. Slipping more and more into a surreal state of mind, I knew how powerfully important Akar's voice had become during the past 50 years on my spiritual journey. Akar's voice was not high pitched or low but rather steady and firm. He frequently spoke to me and guided my eyes in what to look for in an astrology chart while doing readings for my clients. It took many years before I learned the difference between my imagination and Akar (Spirit) talking to me. My thoughts could change back and forth with my mood. Akar was nonnegotiable when he said something. If I didn't get what he was saying he would repeat it and would continue to do so even if he had to say it over and over from one lifetime to the next.

Turning toward my desk to dip my brush into the can of white paint, thoughts of clients I had seen in this very room, or spoke to by phone, flooded my mind.

One client I remember started out with a phone call. I was taking her information over the phone to bill her charge card for the reading when I noticed the address.

"You are only 10 minutes away. Get yourself down here and let me do the reading for you in person," I insisted.

"I will be right there," said the soft Latin voice of a young woman.

I couldn't believe my eyes when I opened the door. The woman I had just talked to was gorgeous. She had long dark hair that cascaded down her back in waves and wore a tight fitting charcoal pant suit with a jacket. Her high heal boots added sophistication and flare.

"Come on in," I greeted.

"I had no idea you were so close," she commented as she followed me to my office.

"What was the date and time of your birth and in what city where you born."

Selma gave me the info and kept talking as I carefully input the data that would be used to calculate her astrology chart.

I turned to respond to something she was asking me when suddenly she was no longer sitting there. In her place was a male sultan. A pure white garment covered his head and draped his body. His piercing black eyes looked like someone had applied eye liner to them to make them stand out even more.

"You look like you saw a ghost," Selma laughed.

"What I saw was your past life," I answered never questioning what the vision was.

"Past life? What do you mean?"

"You were a male sultan clothed in a pure white garment. Your eyes were dark and piercing," I said. "My history is not

5

good enough to know for sure where Sultan's once lived, Persia, maybe, but I know you had a lot of wives."

"The cult. You wouldn't have known," she blurted frantically with inquisitive eyes. "Tell me more about what you saw," she demanded.

"That is all I saw but it was awesome," I smiled.

"The cult," she said again. "I was born the baby of a man who was married to many wives. We were Mormons that got kicked out of the Mormon Church and fled to Mexico. My father was treated like a god and my siblings and I weren't allowed to be around him. Us kids got messed up pretty bad," she sighed looking down. "No one knows about the cult except a counselor I have been seeing. I don't understand who the man was," she added.

"The Sultan was you, Selma," I explained never understanding what she meant by the word cult.

"How could it have been me?"

"What I saw is who you were in a past lifetime. What is remarkable about it is that people who believe in reincarnation believe we come back the opposite of what we were in a past lifetime. For example, if I mistreated blacks in a past lifetime, and there were many who did, I could come back in this lifetime and be of African American decent so I can feel what it is liked being mistreated. But what is so unique about the vision I had, into another dimension and another time, is that you didn't come back the wife but rather the child of a Sultan. There is a word for it, Karma. Karma means coming into this lifetime carrying debts carried over from a past lifetime, whether good or bad."

"I've never heard anything like this before. But I still don't understand why you saw it. No one knows of my past or my family except for the counselor," she repeated.

"I believe it happened because Spirit wanted you to have a recognition symbol, something that would say it was ok for you to trust me."

The reading revealed many things about her and her life thus far. When we were finished she turned to me and said, "I am going to go back home and take these new teachings with me to help my siblings who are still messed up by the life we led."

Strangest thing of all is that I can still see the Sultan so clear in my mind's eye that I can almost reach my hand out and touch his face. He was so handsome.

"I wonder if I am ever going to get done painting these clouds," I thought to myself as I tackled still another one that looked like two people kissing until I dabbed some paint on it so it wouldn't. Their three dimensional form caused you to see different things in them like you would in the sky when cried cry out, "Look at the rabbit hopping along in the sky."

The most bizarre cloud formatting I ever saw was when I was in the car with my sister Betsy and my brother-in-law, Maurice, who was driving. Maurice loved to fish and had even won a couple of boats in competitions he entered. I pointed to the sky and shouted, "Look over there in the sky. It is an enormous fish with a mouth, eyes, and fins," I beamed.

"It sure is," laughed Maurice staring up at it thru the front windshield.

I couldn't bring myself to take my paint and dab out the circle of tribal elders meeting on my wall that were supposed to be conjoining clouds. I needed that good energy and to this day anyone I show it to sees the same thing.

"Tribal elders," I thought to myself. Suddenly, I recalled the time I found a Native American Kachina doll at a Goodwill thrift store. No one finds a Kachina doll at a thrift store but I sure did. It stood about 18 inches tall on a glass case near the cash register where I was going to check out. I immediately put down what I was going to purchase and purchased the hand-painted, hand-carved doll dressed in an authentic ceremonial wardrobe. One of its horns was broken but that didn't keep me from buying it and being overjoyed with the treasurer I had found.

I raced home and started searching through drawers and boxes to try to find something I could use to repair the horn. Then I found a wine cork remover that was made out of wood. The cork remover was brand new. However, it didn't matter that it would be destroyed as long as I was following Akar's guidance. It felt like it was extremely important to restore the Kachina back to what the original artist intended when he carved it. With a sharp steak knife in hand, I carved off a little piece of wood then sanded it down until it was a perfect match for the piece that was missing. When I dabbed my paint brush into some black paint to touch it up something extraordinary happened that was coming from another dimension. I heard Native American chanting in the background. It sounded like a whole nation of Indians urgently crying out to Great Spirit. I loved the rhythm of the sound and I knew from the core of my soul what was really happening. The tribal elders where chanting to me for honoring their customs and for repairing the Kachina doll. Then in a lightning-fast flash, I heard the motor of my refrigerator and found myself saying, "It was good while it lasted but there were no Native American Indians chanting to me. To think such thoughts would make me nuts. It was the refrigerator and my vivid imagination," I laughed disappointedly.

That didn't appear to be the case at all when not long after that incident I got a call from a client who had been listening to a tape recording I made for her.

"Jan," this is Karen. "You are not going to believe what is on a tape that you gave me of our astrology session," she gushed.

"Is there something wrong with the tape?" I asked nervously knowing if something was wrong with the tape I couldn't recreate what Spirit shared with me during the session.

"Nothing is wrong with the tape, quite the opposite," she gushed. "There is Native American chanting going on in the background. Sounds like an entire tribe."

"You have got to be kidding," I said in disbelief remembering the tribal chanting I heard in my home while fixing the Kachina doll. The sound suddenly stopped when I heard the motor humming from my refrigerator and assumed the chanting was in my imagination.

"Have you ever heard Native American chanting in the background on a tape recording of an astrology reading you did for a client," she asked?

"Never," I answered smiling in awe of Spirit and the unseen realm from another dimension that was a form of consciousness that lived long after the elders had died and could tap into my world, apparently, collectively when needed.

As I stood back looking at what a great job I was doing painting the clouds in my office, I realized another time I visually saw another realm that wanted my attention.

It was the time I was reading a book about a Native American medicine man. I was swiftly walking down the sidewalk that lined the parameters of the State Capitol Park when I worked for the Legislature in California. I remember it was hard to go back to my office after having such a peaceful lunch. I heard the bells strike one from a Cathedral nearby. It was then that I saw something in my peripheral vision. To the right of me in the park I thought I could see an enormous coiled snake.

"No time to be thinking about a huge snake that couldn't possibly exist when you're late getting back to work and don't want to get in trouble," my mind reasoned.

"You've been reading a book on Native American traditions. Now when you get a vision you are going to ignore it," shouted Akar in disbelief.

I turned and looked to find where my snake was once coiled there was a large grayish-brown rock of some sort. I walked over to it to see what the snake wanted me to see. I was thinking and talking to myself like a true Native American Indian now. Akar wanted me to see something. Sure enough, it was Indian grinding rocks. Snake wanted me to see the rocks that held the energy of many Native American women who once used their hard surface to crush grains which caused the bowls to form in the rocks. Apparently, the rocks had been brought in to be displayed on the State Capitol grounds.

What I was shown that day actually upset me pretty bad. It was joyful to communicate with Akar and tap into a vision of something communicating from another realm but I knew why it wanted me to see it. Governor Jerry Brown walked thru the Capitol grounds on his way to his apartment almost daily when he was Governor of California the first time. Legislators, staff, and visitors wandered thru the grounds. Benches were placed where people could sit and take in something special exhibits in the park. Most everything had markers and lighting above to highlight what was uniquely there. Not the grinding rocks.

The snake wanted me to see the grinding rocks because I had taken myself into the Native American vibration by reading the book about their traditions at lunch. It wanted me to see what the white man didn't honor. The grinding rocks had a sign but it was very small. To make matters worse the rocks were placed out of sight without a light, or bench for people to sit on like the other exhibits in the park.

Later, everyone I talked to didn't even know the grinding rocks were in the park. I did take the time to write a letter to the State department that's in charge of the Capitol grounds but someone wrote back saying it costs money and it would have to come from the Indians themselves if they wanted to pay for a better marker, a bench, or a light. Then Akar calmed me down by saying, "I just wanted you to see a different dimension and listen to me when I am speaking to you. All that was needed by you has already been done."

"I understand, Akar," I thought to myself.

I could hear the music that was playing in the background, while I painted, come to a stop. It was time to change the CD. I took a rag and lightly touched some white paint then I smeared it on some newsprint. Then I went around making whimsical breezes around my clouds.

"Awesome," my heart shouted out. "Blue skies, white clouds and white trim. Your office really looks fitting for an astrologer to see clients in."

After I changed the CD I brought in the tall glass vase of peacock feathers that stood on the ground. A few marble tables came back into the room. Then I removed the plastic protective drape off the Maple cabinet that showcased hundreds of precious stones I had collected over the years.

I placed two medium sized white quartz singing bowls on two different marble stands. Then I sat the enormous quartz singing bowl that weighed 40 pounds on the cabinet. A young monkey hung from the ceiling over the huge crystal singing bowl. I asked Akar why I was supposed to hang the monkey there that I just purchased from a consignment shop.

"So, you will watch out for the monkey mind" he replied.

"Of course," I thought to myself with a smile on my face. Monkey mind was a Buddhist term I hadn't heard in a long time. Our minds can get restless, unsettled, confused, and uncontrollable. Then we cannot see what is before us. It seemed appropriate that the wood carved Buddha sat close to the monkey.

Akar was always showing me fascinating things about the world I lived in and the powerful forces at play. A perfect example of this was shown to me with the enormous crystal singing bowl sitting beneath the monkey.

On one of my trips to Mt. Shasta I met a woman there named Beverly Ann Wilson at a store called The Crystal Room. Prior to making the trip I spent a lot of time online checking out various stores in Mt. Shasta that carried crystals. When I read about Beverly and her alchemy work with crystal singing bowls I really wanted to meet her.

One day, upon entering her store, I found seven rooms filled with breathtaking art work, jewelry, stained glass, wind chimes, and spirited sculptures. I longed to meet Beverly. It was then that I noticed an older woman with short white hair, bangs pulled back from her pale face, and a rounded body walking towards me.

"Good morning," I smiled recognizing Beverly even though she didn't know me.

"I would like you to come with me. I have something I want to show you," she said smiling. She turned and led me into a private room at the back of the store. She closed the door and said, "Sit down," pointing to the floor.

The room was awesome. There must have been over 80 crystal singing bowls displayed on glass shelves and sitting on the floor close to where she sat down. I had seen the white ones before but many of these bowls were orange, cobalt blue, red, and violet. I knew right away they were specially made for healing the different chakras in the body. Chakras are lights of different colors that can be seen in the etheric body. Each chakra has health areas of the body assigned to it. For example, the fourth chakra is green and it works with the heart. Using a green colored bowl would energetically assist with heart issues whether they be emotional or physical.

Almost an hour flew by as I listened to how Beverly studied to be a Structural Engineer when life took her down a different path when someone placed her in charge of many kilos of crystals that led her to opening up The Crystal Room. Then the talk went deeper when she explained to me the significance of the crystal singing bowls and how they can be used to clear out negative energies, relieve stress, or awaken us to our higher callings.

When I started to leave Beverly looked me straight in the eyes and said, "Spirit told me I was supposed to talk to you today. That is why I brought you back in here and shared what I did."

The journey to Mt. Shasta showed me how powerful the force was when we set our thoughts off on a mission like I did to meet Beverly. She appeared before me without even a phone call other than the one I made mentally that Spirit intercepted. I knew thoughts were powerful but I have long since learned that the key to manifesting anything in our lives was not just the thought but tying our heart to the thought. Feelings rising up from the heart are what ignite the match that brings something about.

After I got home I ordered the enormous white crystal singing bowl then did a little research into it. I found out that our body is made up of millions of crystals. Some of these crystals are called apatite crystals that can be found in our bones, skull and teeth. When the bowl is struck it gives off a haunting sound that resonates with our soul and the crystals in our body. The size of the bowl determines how far the vibration can be felt. My large crystal singing bowl was supposed to resonate for about 5 miles and would normally be used for large gatherings of people.

Now, while still in the vibration of crystals, physically and mentally, something fascinating happened. I was taking a friend of mine to lunch that I hadn't seen in a while and I wanted to take her to some place special. Suddenly, I found myself back on the internet checking out Shingle Springs. I have no clue what my search term on the computer was but suddenly I was learning that a meteorite had exploded over Shingle Springs around 1869 and the Vatican in Rome had a sample of the meteorite in their collection.

I learned there was a metaphysical shop in Shingle Springs that was having a big clearance sale because they were getting ready to move. When my friend and I went to lunch and stopped at the store, I struck up a conversation with a young woman.

"Did you know that a meteorite exploded over Shingle Springs back around 1869?" I asked.

"Never heard that one," she said.

"There is a sample of it in the Vatican in Rome."

"That's interesting. I do know that I have friends around here that pick up crystals in their back yard all the time and think nothing of it."

My jaw dropped. Later that night, when I was all alone, I went back to my computer and learned there were crystal mines between Shingle Springs and Nevada border.

My lesson was that our thoughts ignite the force and while we are in that vibration we will find like vibration whether it is a friend we are thinking about that suddenly calls us for no reason or a bargain we are trying to find when looking for something specific then suddenly it appears at a store we wouldn't normally go to.

I loved my quartz singing bowls. When you strike one bowl right after another they harmonized with each other and make a new sound. My heart was always filled with joy when I let a client play them after a reading and got to see their face light up with excitement.

Chapter 2

I silently sat at my desk looking at the walls of my office knowing that I couldn't have painted the beautiful clouds drifting around the room without the help of Akar guiding me. It was clear to me that my first automobile accident was when I became conscious of a guiding force in my life that was greater than me. However, it was questionable when I actually surrendered to Spirit. For some, the marker in time would be a baptism and for others it would be an epiphany of some sort.

The other thing that was questionable was at what specific point in my life I found myself enrolled in "Spirit School," where it would take a lifetime to graduate from. If the day ever came when I graduated the reward for completing the grueling courses wouldn't be measured in dollars and cents but rather in the extraordinary spiritual gifts I was given of seeing into other dimensions and being able to hear the voice of Spirit through Akar.

There were so many incidences of this happening. I can recall one such time that stands out. It came about when I was working in the Assembly secretarial pool for the California Legislature.

One day I had gone home for lunch like I often did back then but on this particular day I remember picking up the phone and calling my father who lived with my stepmother in Oregon which was an 8 hour drive away from me.

"Hi! Dad," I greeted. My eyes smiled and my heart skipped a beat when I heard my father's voice.

He had always been my hero. As a small child he carried me on top of his shoulders and built me doll houses and a fish pond that I loved. Despite the number of times I thought he was carrying me on his shoulders only to find myself hurling to the ground, disappointed, at something he had done, he still had a special place in my heart that seemed to erase the disappointments and replace them with utter joy.

"Hi! Hon. How are you doing?" He replied with equal excitement causing me to feel a big "love hug," coming through the receiver.

"I called to see how you are doing," I said.

"Things couldn't be better," he responded without hesitation.

"Have you been working in the garden, lately?" I asked.

"You know me well," he laughed. "It's too early to plant the crops but I just walked into the house from tilling the soil in preparation for the spring planting.

"How is mom?" I asked. It was hard calling my stepmother mom because Margie wasn't much older than I was. We got along like sisters when I came to visit but she had snide ways of getting extra attention from my father when I visited like insisting on going out to eat at her favorite place. Yet, I knew my visits meant a lot to her because she was stuck in the wilderness with no friends and my father was miserly tight when it came to spending money which left her with nothing to do but be a field hand and cook. Margie's greatest joy came from my fixing her hair or polishing her nails. She also loved the clothes I always brought her from my closet.

"Oh, she is fine. Margie has been helping me in the garden."

"It's nice to hear your voice. Tell mom I called and tell her Hi for me."

The conversation was sweet and simple like it normally was but as I walked back to work I could feel something wasn't right even though my dad said, "Things couldn't be better." What I felt came from an "all knowing" feeling Akar had taught me to trust without question.

When I got back to work I walked straight into my supervisor's office without even going to my desk first to put down my purse.

"Is everything okay," asked Shirley noticing the concerned look on my face as she turned away from her computer to address me.

"When I went home for lunch I called my father in Oregon. Even though he said everything is fine my gut is telling me something is wrong," I said searching her eyes as if she had the answer.

"No one has more vacation time coming than you do, Jan. Why don't you take a few days off and drive up to Oregon and see your father. It would do you good to get away. Besides, we both know to trust our feelings especially if Spirit is talking to us or trying to show us something."

Shirley was like my spiritual musketeer. Even though she was my supervisor I had shared many lunch hours with her in her office while we talked about astrology and other metaphysical subjects or shared interesting things we were learning in books we read.

"Thanks, Shirley. I am going to take you up on your offer and take tomorrow off and drive up there. Maybe nothing is wrong and I just need to see my dad. I will be back in three days."

I got up before the Sun came up and hit the road while most people were still sleeping. Even though I was fresh and wide awake I found myself getting sleepy eyed after 2 hours of nothing to look at except one farm field after another whipping past as I drove by them. Once I reached Redding the mountains offered winding rivers with rapids splashing over river rocks for me to see.

Suddenly, I saw my old friend who always towered high above the other mountains as if it were trying to touch the sky. A smile came to my face. It was Mt. Shasta wearing a blanket of white snow that beautifully contrasted the deep blue sky. I rolled down the window to take a breath of the crisp cold air. It would be another hour before I would come to a town called Mt. Shasta City that lay at the foot of the Mountain. In the meantime watching my friend peek behind turns as I drove through the mountains entertained me and kept me from feeling tired anymore.

Five more hours of continuous driving passed before I arrived at the white mail box that marked the turnoff to my dad's home. His home was not bigger than a small wood cabin but instead of beautiful wooden logs it had rose shingles and a pale green roof worn with age. What gave the property its charm was the river running behind the home with a mountain towering above it, blanketed with enormous green pine trees.

"Rough. Rough…Rough!" warned Rex. But his wagging tail showed his warning wasn't too sincere when he saw it was me getting out of the car.

"Hi Darlin," greeted Margie in surprise, with a toothless smile and long dark hair that framed her round face. She was wearing a cotton print robe that snapped up the front revealing a flat chest which meant she was also not wearing a bra. Although it was almost 4:00 pm, I had caught her off guard without wearing her false teeth and her hair was uncombed.

"Hi Mom," I said setting down a small suitcase and giving her a hug.

"You never told us you were coming," she said with her back to me as she hurried across the room to a glass on the coffee table. She reached in a grabbed her false teeth then turned around looking ten years younger.

"Have a seat," she gestured with her hand towards the sofa.

"Where's dad?" I asked looking around for him.

"He's not here," she said. "He drove up to the VA Hospital in Roseburg this morning."

"Hospital," I mocked looking alarmed.

"He's ok," she said. "He went up there to have some cancers removed."

"What cancer?" I asked. "When I talked to him on the phone yesterday he said everything was fine and couldn't be better."

"That was just your dad's way of keeping you from worrying. He knows you have an important job in Sacramento."

"Where was the cancer?" I repeated.

"There was a spot on his left ear and another larger one on his back that they were going to remove."

"He told me on the phone that everything couldn't be better but I just knew something was wrong so I asked my supervisor for a couple of days off so I could come out and check on both of you for myself," I explained.

"That was mighty nice of you. He'll be so surprised you are here when he gets home."

Just then I heard Rex, their old golden-haired German Shepard barking. He was a pup when my dad got him. I also heard tire wheels racing down the gravel road.

"That must be Herman now," said Margie.

I turned back the curtain behind me and peeked out the picture window to see the headlights of my dad's SUV headed towards the house.

"Yes. Its dad," I smiled, turning my body to face Margie.

"Hi! Hon," shouted my dad when he opened the door and our smiling eyes met.

"Hi, Dad," I raced towards him to get my big bear hug.

"How did you know something was wrong? I never said anything when we talked on the phone."

"I just missed you and wanted to see you," I beamed looking up at the tall man I adored that was a country farmer, normally attired in jean overalls and a white holey tee shirt. Today, he wore slacks and a nice white shirt that matched the bandage on his left ear. When I hugged him back I was careful not to hurt the surgical wound that I could tell he was favoring on the left side of his back.

I never let on that Akar (a Spirit guide that I could not see) literally said, "Leave at once and go see your father," with words that were not audible to anyone else in this world but me.

My visit was three fold. I was always able to cheer up my stepmother, Margie, who sometimes got depressed living on the farm so far away from people. It cheered up my father who always treated me like a celebrity in front of his friends. And the trip gave me a chance to escape the pressures I faced working for the Legislature at the State Capitol where most jobs that needed to be done were due the day before they were given to you.

Talks with my dad by the stream and eating delicious southern food Margie prepared as good as any master chef was delightful but it caused the days to fly by before it was finally time to say goodbye.

Rex was the first to say goodbye as he jumped up on me so I would pat him on his head.

"Drive safe, Hon," my dad whispered to me as we hugged.

"I hate to see you go," said Margie with tears in her eyes.

"You all take care now," I said closing the car door behind me.

It was still dark and the journey was quiet. When the Sun rose I could once again see tree lined roads with creeks appearing around the bends as my car drove up and down tall curvy mountains. In the distance was a mother deer with a fawn by her side grazing in the forest. Birds were perched on fence posts. The peaceful surroundings put me into a tranquil state of mind. I found my thoughts wandering off to Akar.

I thought to myself, "Wow," my father sounded so cheerful on the phone the day I called him on my lunch hour. But Akar knew what was going on and wanted me to go see him."

I never mentioned to my father that Akar was responsible for my coming to visit him. Margie and dad never knew about my spirit guide but they had both experienced the results of things I had seen or heard from another dimension. For example, one morning I called Margie upset about something I dreamed. In it I saw a coffin and my grandmother which caused me to think someone in the family had died. My stepmother told me no one had died and that she and my grandmother had just been talking on the phone the day before about Uncle Lee Roy.

Two days later, Margie called me sounding frantic. Apparently, my Uncle Lee Roy had committed suicide and was writing a note to my father, his brother, while I was dreaming it. The bizarre thing that I never understood about this is that this uncle had molested me when I was a young child. It was unfortunate because he was my favorite uncle who always brought me fantastic toys when he came to visit.

After several years had passed of not seeing this uncle since I was a child, I developed into an attractive teenager with blue eyes, long blonde hair, and a shapely body. When I went to visit my father, one summer, my uncle was there. The look I saw in my uncle's eyes when he looked at me was that of a child gazing on a scrumptious piece of candy it had to have in a candy store. When our eyes met I was drawn to him in a mysterious way I couldn't explain that caused me to seductively flirt with him while constantly looking around to make sure no one was looking. It was one of those dark secrets that made no sense but had caused a lot of guilt at the time.

But why in the world would his thoughts of killing himself, and actually doing it, travel straight to me in my dream while he was writing the note to my dad? I wondered if the answer to his and my connection was in reincarnation. Had we known each other in a past lifetime and what role did we play in each other's lives back then?

There were many other incidences of things that happened that were memorable but difficult to explain. One time when I was visiting, I was sitting in the car with Margie waiting for my dad to come and drive us to town. Going to town was always a treat because they didn't do it very often. Apparently, my father was searching for the lid to a gas can that he couldn't find. He needed to find it so he could buy some gas for his tractor which happened to be the reason we were going to town in the first place.

I got out of the car and walked back to his garage. We looked and looked but we couldn't find it. Finally, I released the desperate feeling I had from not finding it and turned the search over to Akar.

"Where is the lid?" I asked calmly never expecting a response.

"Check the tractor, I heard my spirit guide say.

"I already checked the tractor," I responded annoyed.

"Under the tire," said Akar.

I stomped off to look under one of the huge tires belonging to the tractor. Sitting on the ground beneath the wheel, out of sight, was the lid. I sensed Akar was laughing.

Trying to make sense of things that had happened in my life that were difficult to understand always made me feel like I was working on a big jig saw puzzle that would reveal my life's purpose if I could find the final piece. Back then, such thoughts only served to help the hours pass on my trip back home from visiting my dad.

However, I remember, something else unexpectedly happened that day with Akar's signature on it. I had stopped in Grants Pass, Oregon to shop in a few stores and have some lunch to break up the monotony of the long trip home. Several hours later, I got back on the road not realizing I was about to be presented with another test from the "Spirit School" I found myself enrolled in.

It happened 5 miles before the exit to the City of Mt. Shasta in California. I found myself searching for the enormous snow-capped mountain as my car whipped around the bends. If you wanted to see the artistic talents of God, Divine Mother, Christ, Universe, Saints of all religions, Great Spirit, you would see it when you looked up and gazed at Mt. Shasta. Mt. Shasta was originally a volcano that erupted hundreds of years ago spewing hot lava over the entire area.

The serenity of the trees passing by caused me to stop admiring the Mountain when I did see it. Instead, I started listening to the words in my minds ear.

"Stop at Mt. Shasta and go to the bookstore and buy a book on color healing, said Akar."

"I am not stopping at Mt. Shasta," I answered.

"Stop at Mt. Shasta and go to the bookstore," came the monotone but firm voice.

"It is Sunday, the book store is closed," I countered.

"Stop…"

"No, it is 4:30 pm and if the store was open it is closed now."

"Stop at the bookstore in Mt. Shasta."

The final exit sign appeared before me which read, Exit Mt. Shasta City.

I was tired after driving for so long but the gas tank was getting low so I thought I would GO TO THE BOOKSTORE to prove it was closed or maybe even out of business, then buy gas.

My car came to a stop in the parking lot below the bookstore that was housed on the second story of a building with wood siding.

I climbed up the steps, annoyed with Spirit and the Goose chases it took me on, until I reached the door of the store. There was a red sign on the door with the letters OPEN on it.

"Okay. Okay. Akar, you were right the store is open," I snapped shrugging my shoulders.

"Do you have any books on color healing?" I asked the young male attendant with brown bangs combed to the side of his fair skinned face.

"Normally, we have books on color healing," he said. "But we are all out of them right now."

"Ah! Ha!" I proclaimed joyfully to Akar which I assumed was walking in with me. "Gotcha…Gotcha…Gotcha," I chuckled to myself. "It was worth the stop," I sported a smug smile that was visible for people to see, and question.

I walked to a round table of books in the center of the store then reached for this huge book that was wider than it was tall and read the title, COLOR HEALING.

"You got to be kidding," I told myself. Akar was right about everything; the store being open on Sunday, open that hour of the day, and that there would be a book on color healing.

That experience stayed with me all these years. It was remarkable that I was directed to go see my father in the first place who sounded like he was well and happy on the phone. When you added that Akar had gone ahead of me on the road, knew the store was open, and found the book that I was guided to reach for when I walked into the store; it was a lot to take in.

Nonetheless, it was a drop in the bucket in comparison with what I would learn from Akar in the days that followed, more lessons, more tests administered from another dimension in a world I could not see but it was a class or a school that anyone could attend if they got quiet and listened to the chatter in their minds and learned to sort it out.

Chapter 3

One night, many years ago, sitting alone in a hot tub, I gazed upon the black velvet sky above me sprinkled with sparkling diamonds that were a mixture of the stars and planets that made up my world as an astrologer. Feeling as though I was in a trance that had been induced from the serenity of the heavens my eyes studied and the warmth of the in which water I sat, I knew it was time for me to ask my guide, known only to me as the voice of Spirit, "What is your name?"

"AKAR," echoed the heavens, which sent goose bumps trickling down my spine that were more piercing than the cool night breeze.

"What do you look like?" I asked, eager to know what this energy force was that had manifested itself into my life with all kinds of demands on me and with which I sometimes argued to no avail. Other times, I just laughed to myself when I got the point that this unknown force was trying to show me.

"I am in your world, but I am not of it. I cannot be Caucasian, Asian, Latino, African American or Native American; I am not an Irish pickpocket, nor any other human tag with which you are familiar. I am Akar, form without form, such as flowing water, the sound of 'aa' in music, or OM, the living energy -- at one with the greatest life force that has ever existed."

I was silent for a moment. As I gazed at a shooting star passing over, I knew the one that had been guiding me, for whom I had such a deep love, and with whom I was speaking now, was a holy divine force. For years people had told me the name of their guides and gave them ethnic characteristics, beards, and penetrating eyes, but my guide was nameless until now. Nonetheless, I knew Akar represented God, Divine Mother, Christ, Spirit, Saints of all religions, Great Spirit, Universe, and any name of an unseen Divine Force.

"Why haven't you ever told me your name before now?" I questioned ever so humbly.

"You never asked," echoed the familiar firm voice.

It was then that I first realized the difference between my mental babble and my guide whom I now knew as Akar. The difference was that the babble was unsteady and left me with a feeling of uncertainty. Akar never wavered. What he said was non-negotiable. If I didn't do what he asked, he asked again, and again, and again, until I did, never judging me, never angry. And if I didn't do as I was asked, I knew he would have continued to ask me from one lifetime to the next until I did.

It would take years clumped in 10's before I would understand that Spirit was no more than a Divine Force of consciousness.

Each of us has access to a Divine consciousness that can take us into a magical world that has answers to all of our questions and will let us see into the future.

Each of us has a Spirit guide that can freely move forward ahead of us to see what lurks. The guide can also see behind us and cover our backs with a warning or a feeling that will cause us to turn around or head down a different path. Though this force is unseen and its source is rooted in another dimension, it is present for all of us. Furthermore, this guide stays awake while a person is asleep and can travel across town or across the world to see what is happening that may affect the human soul they are guiding.

All these things were what Akar showed me when I attended "Spirit School."

I neither knew when my lessons began, nor did I realize the drama I was living at any given time was about to be followed by one of Akar's exams. Sometimes, the exam wouldn't come for years. Often times, the test appeared in my life like leaving a bad relationship only to attract the same type of person the second time around. It took many years before Akar showed me I was attracting older men in my life to try and win the approval of my father. Eventually, I recognized this and wasn't attracted to older men anymore. I passed this test when I learned to love me for me rather than needing someone else to heal the wounds of my inner child.

Other tests related to money. When I was younger, I would face situations where I was spending too much money, getting myself in debt, and worrying about it all night, but when the same type of situation would happened years later, I knew I could go online and sell some stuff on Ebay and didn't have to worry about money.

Some of my life lessons were brutal, and in order to get to where I am now with peace of mind and feeling as though I lack for nothing, it meant occasionally wandering off the path I was on and walking into a dark forest where evil creatures lurk, and witches want to possess my soul. I soul-tweaked those universes I visited on other dimensions and sometimes I barely escaped with my life and didn't know how deep into the forest I had wandered.

Early on, I learned the power of thoughts and how it is our thoughts that project a powerful energy that moves the sails that guide us forward to face whatever demons, work situation, money, etc., we created by what we were thinking. In other words, my thoughts could be powerful. How cool ʼʰⁿt knowingness? WRONG.

Akar was quiet, or I wasn't listening when I found myself being tested in another mess. At work, I got caught in a political trap of such magnitude other people simply can't even imagine.

One day, I was helping out in a Legislator's office. I play that down a bit. It was actually Doris Allan's office. She briefly took over as Speaker for the California State Assembly.

I don't know how I managed to do it, but I always was in a key place when something was going down politically inside the State Capitol. It didn't matter if it was riding the elevator with Arnold Schwarzenegger prior to his being elected Governor or transcribing a tape when Bishop Tutu or Butalizi was visiting. I can still remember Prince Phillip saying, "Hi!" and smiling at me as I returned the smile and said, "Hi!" back as he and Queen Elizabeth passed by where I was standing in the rotunda on the second floor of the State Capitol Building. She was surrounded by Sergeant-at-Arms who was protecting her as she waved and spoke to the crowds below from behind a bullet-proof shield.

Anyway, while I was in Doris' office a gentleman wearing a blue suit and tie came to see me.

"How would you like to come to work for the Cost Control Commission in the Senate?" he asked.

I had never considered working for the Senate at all let alone a commission about which I had never heard.

"If you get caught in a political war that is being waged, your back will be covered. I would like you to come with me and meet the consultant to the commission who has asked me to come and talk to you," the lean man with dark hair added.

"Political wars?" I thought to myself. I did my job. I made it a point not to buy into what went on around me, and I had a reputation for being damn good at what I did as a Committee Secretary for the Democrats. However, he was right. The wars had already begun. The Republicans had taken over the House and were now in power, which meant the Democratic chairmen had to step down from their committees. The takeover cost me my job, and now the Secretarial Pool in which I was hiding out until I could find something else was in threat of being dissolved.

I got up and excused myself from the office in which I was working and followed the young man thru a tunnel that led to a couple of offices that were separated from the mainstream of legislative offices in the new building. The tunnel marked the separation between the old building of the State Capitol and the new building that was added many years after the original structure was built when the Legislature outgrew itself. I had worked in the office he was guiding me towards before and always liked it because of the skylights in the ceiling that allowed me to see clouds passing by blue skies.

When I walked into the office, I expected to see the legislator sitting behind his desk that I remembered from having helped out in his office before. Instead, the chair was empty. Sitting on the sofa was a man whose energy wreaked that of WARRIOR. He was Hispanic, and he had short wavy jet-black hair with dark piercing eyes. Behind the warrior energy I felt I should be careful of his smile that lit up his eyes.

"I am so glad you could come," he stood up and extended his hand for me to shake it. Then, he motioned for me to sit in the chair close by.

"I don't know how much you were told prior to coming here. Jill, the secretary here, has highly recommended you for the work you have done with her in the past," he smiled. "I've never needed a secretary before, but the Commission for which I am working has grown, and I find myself getting bogged down with work."

"What type of work would I be doing, and how hard is it to cross over from the Assembly to the Senate?" I asked.

"You would be doing work similar to what you are doing now. The main thing I need is to have the office covered when I am out meeting with legislators or at other meetings. There are 25 commissioners that sit on the commission for whom you would be working that live all over California. When we have a hearing, I will need you to help me set it up, which entails notifying them, getting materials typed up and printed, along with securing a room somewhere in the State Capitol. You will also need to make arrangements for a lunch that will be catered to your specifications.

"I haven't done catering before, but it shouldn't be a problem," I responded.

"Your salary will remain the same as it is now. One more thing, I will protect you if the political wars threaten you in anyway. I promise that," he said with eyes, warning me that there were things happening about which he knew but that I didn't.

"As far as transferring from the Assembly to the Senate, it is just paperwork. You will still get credit for the years you have worked in the Assembly if you are in the retirement system."

"I've worked here for a little over 26 years and am just now paying back my retirement system. So, I am glad to hear I will still get credit for those years, and it will just continue on if I transfer to the Senate.

"Does this mean you will take the job?" he asked, carefully studying my eyes.

"Yes, I will come to work for you," I said hesitantly. "When would you like for me to start?"

"Immediately," he answered.

I went back to the office where I was working and told them I was leaving and when I mentioned the name of the man I would be working for their jaws dropped.

Well, things aren't always as they appear. This person had no authority to hire me in the first place let alone to make promises about protecting me if I got caught in political wars. It also turned out it that it was his hide that the Democrats were after and the Republicans were after it, too. This guy was so powerful that he helped write the House rules which most legislators were not qualified to do. He was well known for running the campaigns of many elected officials, and once ran for office himself but didn't win.

After leaving the Assembly and making a pledge to the Senate, I found out my job was not secure because my being hired hadn't cleared proper channels. Instead, I took a salary cut of $800 a month and at times found myself alone at home in my condo, wondering whether or not this person, who I cannot name, was going to get everything straightened out like he had promised.

It was then that I walked into the dark forest without realizing I had wandered off my well lit path in search of power that I had lost and relinquished. I needed power to restore my money and to secure my job, so I wouldn't lose my condo or my retirement that I had been working so hard to secure.

As I considered my plight, I remembered that I had once spent my time studying the Kabbalah and communicating with an entity in one of its Sephiroth's. But the Kabbalah took a lifetime to learn how to use its powers. I needed help now, and it had to come from me.

I had been studying a book on magic that claimed we all had power within us that we could access at any time. In it, the author said I could close my eyes and visualize that I was in a forest, so I did. Next, I imagined a castle behind some trees. I walked up to the enormous wooden doors and knocked, but no one answered. I gripped the iron handle with both hands and pulled the door open. Inside was an enormous room. As I turned around, I could see many doors with emblems on them that led to other rooms, but I didn't try to go in them. There was also a fountain standing in the middle of the room.

My focus immediately went to the fountain. Towering above the fountain was a ceiling made of glass that revealed twinkling stars and a bright full moon. I remember writing something in this fountain that was like a tall birdbath that came to my waist. It resembled an abyss where something blue was there, but it wasn't of this world, nor was it really water. I took my finger and spelled the words MONEY that left a trail of white smoke as if it were coming from a crop duster.

Looking back, I laugh knowing Akar must have also been laughing at my foolishness. I wanted to manifest money and have the power to do it. Somehow, I wasn't even aware of my leaving a brightly lit path in life until I found myself in the castle I manifested in my mind that day -- a castle with symbols on doors and an abyss that could have been a cauldron reeking with hoodoo, voodoo, and magic. It was all just a game to entertain me and give me power and control over my life where I needed it most ... with money. Like an innocent child smelling warm cookies, I played on without realizing the consequences.

Next, in my mind I transformed the ethereal mass on which I had been writing into water that rose higher and higher and higher until it almost touched the top of the castle in which I stood. Then I let the water in which I wrote the words, "Money, money, money," fall. Suddenly, when I looked up to the ceiling, I saw the fountain instantly change into green bills of money, falling from above.

I walked away from that experience thinking that at the very least I learned I could mentally manifest a castle with something that looked like water in it, one that had magical doors -- not to mention a whole forest with money falling down all around me from the ceiling. How cool was that?

As SPIRIT is my witness, (forget about Akar), I could never have dreamed what followed, nor did I ever tell a soul about what I had mentally manifested until now.

Two weeks later, after playing like an innocent child in the forbidden castle, something bizarre happened. I was driving to work one morning. It was like any other morning with too many cars on the road. all racing to get to work before the clock struck the magic hour when everyone was supposed to be at work.

Suddenly, an enormous red Peterbilt truck, carrying the energy of the Devil himself, was changing lanes and headed towards the side of my vehicle. Fear raced through me when I was near trucks because their hard metal bodies had hurt me before in accidents when I was driving. Then, it came; I felt the crushing impact of the truck, which sent my car spinning out of control. In my mind, I feared the car would tip over into the ditch on the side of the road although looking at the site years later, there was no ditch.

It was in that moment, inside the spinning vehicle, that I experienced two things happening. One, I was mentally looking up at money falling down on me from above just like what I had seen a few weeks prior when I wrote the word, "MONEY," in the abyss and then the words rose up towards the ceiling of the castle.

"That was then, but this was now," I told myself. Yet, it was the same vision. For a split second, while the car spun out of control, I knew I had created the accident. And it was a bad one. The fascia, a connective tissue that encases our body, was torn in my back. For many years, whenever I would walk in cold weather it felt as though I was being stabbed in my back with a thousand knives.

The second thing that happened that day is while the car was spinning out of control (it actually spun around and was facing four lanes of rush hour traffic, now headed towards me), I could feel my body being held in something like an enormous soft leather baseball glove. The love directed towards me from whoever was holding me exceeded any love I have ever known. For the first time since I was born to this existence on Earth, I knew I didn't have to worry about my body or what was going to happen to me. It was a feeling I didn't want to let go of – I wanted to just stay in that moment a little bit longer.

When my children and loved ones flashed before my mind, I had no concern for them because I knew whatever this FORCE was that was protecting me and loving me now, it would be there for them as well -- if they only let it. Apparently, I was having a near death experience. It wasn't until then that I realized how I always had to look after my body, i.e., feed it, exercise it, move it, and make it sleep. For a brief moment, I knew I could trust the FORCE that was taking responsibility for my body, and the burden was no longer mine.

I looked up to see four lanes of traffic facing me. My tires left black skid marks on the road, revealing the fact that I had been dragged hundreds of feet. Some men pushed my car to the side of the road with it still facing the opposite direction from which I was traveling. While sitting there, I felt fire explode at the base of my spine. My back was already weak from the time a truck hit my car, which brought my spirit guide Akar, into my life when it was raining, and he asked me to roll down my windshield before I got hit.

I took a piece of paper from my purse and a pen to write down the name of a Native American woman who was standing near me. My pen wouldn't make the letters that my mind knew it should.

"You are in shock," spoke the soft voice of the thin olive-skinned woman with long dark hair pulled back from her face in a ponytail.

I looked at her as I tried to make sense of what had happened.

"I can't write."

"I know. You are in shock. You've been in a car accident."

Finally, I was able to write her Native American name down, which I don't remember anymore.

She said she was told by Spirit that morning in the mountains, when she was driving in from Lake Tahoe, that there was going to be an accident up ahead.

"Did you hear me singing the Native American Shaman's Healing song to you a few minutes ago?" she asked.

"No," I responded barely able to stand and support my back.

It took a year to receive the cash settlement for all the time I was off work and the injuries I sustained. I never mentioned my ceremony to the attorney, nor did I discuss the dark forest and maybe innocent witch craft or magic with which I was playing from my toy box. I wasn't sure how that information would have affected the case other than to make my attorney and others want to lock me up in a loony tune bin somewhere.

A few months later, I went to see the man who was a warlock, a warlock that I -- somehow -- had managed to manifest into coming to my life six months prior to the accident. Back then, I got it into my mind that I wanted to meet a witch. Next thing I knew, I was off the beaten path I normally followed, stopping at a feed store where two half-dressed young children were running around eating ice cream for breakfast. I saw a man sitting behind some display cases at a computer in the corner of the store.

I walked towards him and noticed that he was writing a book. I sat down, and we carried on a conversation for over an hour before I left. Our conversation revealed that he was the leader of the Wicca organization in Sacramento. When we finished talking, I raced home and found the video tape that the man, who looked like a goat with wiry long reddish uncombed hair and porous skin, had mentioned that he had loved but said he couldn't find among his own possessions. I knew the power of thoughts, and I wanted to break our connection. I felt giving him the tape would do that and be a way to thank him for his time.

The name of the movie was **Resurrection**. It was a 1980 film, starring Ellen Burstyn, which tells the story of a woman who lives through a car accident that kills her husband. She learns she has the power to heal others.

I don't know if the man in the feed store was a witch or a warlock, but he was sure surprised when I walked back in the store a short time later and practically threw the movie his way before racing out of the store.

When I went back to see him after the accident, I really wanted to know what went wrong. I was no witch, nor did I want to become one -- quite the contrary, in fact. However, I knew this man -- who professed to be a witch/warlock and who sold a lot of tiny clear bags filled with things labeled, "Dragon's Blood, Mugwort, and Eyes of Newt," in the back of that feed store -- might have some answers for me. After all, don't witches cast spells and conjure things up? I knew I surely conjured up the accident, but I wasn't a witch. I was just a woman who needed answers.

So, I asked him, "I needed money. My salary was cut pretty badly, and I was barely making ends meet. So, I did this mental ceremony where money was falling from the top of a castle all over me. A few days later, I was in a bad auto accident, and I saw the same thing I envisioned in the ceremony. Money was falling down upon me. I must have created the accident. What went wrong?" I quizzed him with my brows wrinkled.

"Rule one," he said. "You only ask for what you need. You said 'Give me money,' but you didn't specify how much."

"Oh," I responded. "Of course you should only ask for what you need."

There was only one other time I saw him again. It was about a year later when two young women were spending a lot of time with me, trying to tweak their spiritual journeys.

"Do you want to meet a witch?" I asked with a devilish smile.

"Oh yes," they said, shaking their heads affirmatively up and down with excitement.

"Grab your purses. Off we go."

The eyes of the young women were wide open as we walked into the feed store.

"I would like you to meet my friends," I told the old man.

"How do you do?" he said with his goat-like face, wiry hair, big nose, and unbathed body, revealing a few missing teeth.

"Hello," they answered, backing up as they pretended to peruse the exotic Wiccan herbs on display in back of the store.

When we got back into the car, both of them were frightened and scared of him. They told me they wanted no part of him let alone to have a conversation with a man that looked like a beast.

"You can learn from a goat," I mused. "If I were afraid of him and didn't know where my beliefs were rooted, then I wouldn't have learned the things he shared with me."

Next, I took them to a nice little candle shop a couple of blocks away, so they could feel the positive energy of the young woman who ran the store. I don't recall them asking any questions about the voodoo candles that were lurking in the back corner of this store.

These were just some of the lessons offered by the "Spirit School," for which some unknown someone had enrolled me without my knowing it.

The dark forests I sometimes found myself in were scary. The pain was sometimes brutal. And despite all I had been through, the lessons would go on.

Chapter 4

I watched the two young women laughing and talking as they left heading to their parked cars. Chuckling to myself, I closed the door behind me and walked down the hall covered in jungle murals towards my office.

A fake zebra rug runner lay on the floor, giving added ambience to the scenes I had painted. I knew these paintings represented a past life I once lived where my skin was silky black, wild animals roamed freely, and ceremonies were rooted in family traditions.

Looking at the murals reminded me of when I left California to go work for the State Department in Washington, D.C. Time seemed to stand still as I waited for almost a year to get my security clearance, so I could go work in an embassy in Africa.

Countless times over the years, I would see pictures of Africa, and tears would come to my eyes. Once, after having lunch at the Virgin Sturgeon that was located on the banks of the American River, someone was talking to me, but I couldn't hear a word. My eyes locked in on a tree that stood tall on the other side of the river. My heart swelled, and I became very emotional. For a brief second, the tree changed and became a blackened silhouette against the autumn colored sky that darkened as the sun set. But it wasn't evening; it was midday. Without question, I knew my soul remembered a previous lifetime when I stood watching the same sunset.

The State Department turned out to be a bad idea. I didn't like the stories I was hearing from women who had worked in the embassies. The military service men would search their desks when they were taking dictation from their Ambassador, and then give them demerits if they had left something classified in the open. Consulate training left me looking for microfilm in my sleep between my sheets for fear I was going to get caught having lost it. The story one woman told of having fun finding ways to conceal alcohol, so that she could take a drink now and then helped to paint a picture of lonely women who never got married and who traveled around the world without a place to call home. I would need a drink, too. Eventually, I quit my job and caught the next plane headed for California.

I sat down at my desk in my office and again thought of the goat-faced man who practiced Wicca and Malanga, the lovely black woman who ran the candle store. What the two young women who had gone with me to both locations earlier that day didn't know is the fact that at one time I myself had owned several of the books that were for sale in the candle store. One book I remember was called, "Candle Magic." That book led me to taking a class Malanga taught on candle burning and magic in the evenings when it was dark. The sign on the counter that announced the class look pretty innocent, so I signed up for it never realizing how naïve I really was.

In my way of thinking, magic from ceremonies was something a person learned by the time they were two years old. When a child bends over a birthday cake, they make a wish (intent) and then blow out the candles, sending their wish into the ethers. At that age, they are too young to know that the longer we hold our breath and think about our wish before blowing out the candle the more it will strengthen our wish.

On my way to the candle shop to take the class, I recalled several times in my life when I burned candles that yielded amazing results. The one that stood out the most was the time I walked across the street from the State Capitol to the Cathedral of the Blessed Sacrament Catholic Church in the heart of downtown Sacramento. I was six months pregnant, didn't have a job, and had no place to turn. I pushed open two giant mahogany doors.

I quietly walked along the rows of benches where people sat praying as I studied stained glass windows and life-sized statues mounted on the walls that towered over me. Turning into a small alcove, I saw many candles flickering in red glass votive candle holders. Again, to me it was just a candle that sat in a sacred sanctuary. White was the color for purity or peace. The color red represented love or the heart. I put twenty-five cents in the small metal box mounted on the wall next to the candles, which clanked when it dropped. Then, I took a match, lit one candle, and said a prayer, which was really making a wish. Then, I walked over to St. Anthony, holding a child.

"Please help me," I pleaded. "I have nowhere to go, and I, too, am carrying a child." Tears came to my eyes as I began to sob.

Within twenty-four hours, I received a phone call that answered my prayers.

"Hello," I said.

"Hi, Jan. You don't know me, but I am your mom's friend. My name is Ray.

"My mother?"

"Yes. She called me worried about you. Your stepfather would never let her help you, so I will on behalf of your mother, who has been a dear friend of mine for a long time."

"I don't understand," I said.

"She said you were pregnant and didn't have anywhere to go. I have booked a flight for you to come to San Diego. Once you get here, we will get some aid somewhere to help you, but I need you to be here, so I can help."

"You don't even know me," I said.

"I owe your mother a favor for something she once did for me. We will just let it go at that," he replied.

"When am I supposed to fly down there?"

"Tomorrow morning. I will be waiting for you at the airport."

Twenty-five cents, a match to a candle, and a wish -- suddenly, my obstacle vanished.

Still looking back to my candle burning class, I remember looking around the room and studying the people who attended the class. I counted eight people. They were different ages. My heart skipped a beat when I noticed one gorgeous chocolate-skinned man with piercing dreamy eyes who was looking right at me. I smiled, but whenever I turned to look towards him as we sat in the back of the room, our eyes met, and it felt like our souls touched and remembered something long forgotten. He turned out to be Malanga's husband.

My energy was no match for the powerful energy coming from Malanga's husband. He knew things that only life experiences could have taught him. Candles for me were like lollypops to a child in comparison to what this man and his wife, Malanga, knew.

However, candles would talk to me and take me into other dimensions. That reason alone is why the class interested me. A perfect example of candles talking to me was when a prominent political figure for whom I had read astrology charts learned through a friend that I sometimes burned candles and prayed for someone who needed it. So, he called me.

"Hi, Jan," he said as I recognized the voice from previous readings I had done and interviews I had seen of him on the media. "This is Charles."

"Hi, Charles. What can I do for you?" I asked curiously.

"It's not about me, Jan. I am calling about my father," he said softly.

"Your father? What would you like to know about your father, Charles?" I questioned.

"He's sick and has to have surgery. Could you glance at his astrology chart and see if you see anything?" he hedged.

"Of course," I said, writing down his father's birth information. "I will draw up the astrology chart and then call you back," I added.

I took the information and fed it into my computer; then, I studied where the planets were at birth and where they were now.

"Hi, Charles," I greeted him when the receiver was picked up.

"Hi, Jan. I didn't expect you to call so soon, but I am glad you did," he said appreciatively.

"Your father's astrology chart tells me that this is a heavy time for him. I see a wall that won't come down for ten days. He must get past this wall, which represents difficult aspects amongst malefic planets that have him cornered like battleships at sea right now. Once he gets past the wall, he will be fine," I assured.

"Thank you so much. I heard you sometimes burn candles for people. Would you please burn one for my father?" he asked.

"Of course I will. I would be honored to do so."

"Thank you, Jan. I'll be talking to you soon," he said before hanging up.

I really did feel honored that Charles wanted me to burn a candle for his father. In books I had read on candle burning, I knew the energy was stronger when a person handmade the candle or placed herbs in the melted wax. So, I thought I would try this method. I wouldn't use bee's wax because I didn't have any, but I knew bee's wax was even more powerful because the energy of the bees remains in the wax they make.

A quick trip to a Goodwill thrift store turned up all the supplies I needed without costing much money; I bought items like aluminum pans to melt the wax, a votive candle holder, and a measuring cup.

I went to my computer and looked up what herbs holistic folks or witches were using for peace and healing. The three herbs I chose were: basil for calming a person and easing muscle spasms, cayenne because it would relieve pain and reduce phlegm in the lungs after surgery, and lemon balm for love, healing, and peace.

I held thoughts of Charles' father and his upcoming surgery close to my heart throughout the process. I crushed herbs and melted the pure white wax. I took the scissors and shortened a candle wick that was attached to a flat metal piece that held it in place when it dropped to the bottom of the clear votive candle holder. When the melted wax was poured, I sprinkled in the crushed herbs.

Next, I placed the candle on top of a metal filing cabinet at the corner of my office that had a few stones nearby and a small cobalt blue vase of fresh-picked fragrant white Gardenias. I closed my eyes and said, "God, I am not praying for outcomes here. I am only asking for peace while this man faces what is ahead for him according to your divine will."

I went about tidying up the kitchen before going out into my patio and trimming my herbs that were growing in a cut wooden wine barrel. Then, I walked into the house towards my office to see how the candle was burning.

"Oh, my," I gasped, not believing my eyes as a horrible feeling went over me -- one of fear touching my soul. "Something is not right," I thought to myself as I studied the wick that had turned itself under as if forming a fist. The herbs had come together and looked like coagulated red blood at the base of the wick.

"It is just your imagination, Jan," I reasoned. "Nothing is wrong. It is just a candle, you Drama Queen."

A few days later, I answered the phone at work.

"Hi, Jan," gushed Charles with excitement. "I am glad you answered the phone. I was calling to talk to your boss, but before I do, I want to thank you for what you did for my father when you read his chart for me and burned a candle."

"Hi, Charles. How is your father doing?" I asked hesitantly.

"He couldn't be better. The surgery went fantastic. He sailed through it like a champ and was flirting with the nurses in the hospital when I left him this morning," he said.

"The wall, Charles," I gently cautioned him. I didn't want to let the air out of his balloon. "Your father has two or three days before he is out of the woods," I added reluctantly. I knew the wall. That wall occurs when transiting malefic planets are locked into birth planets, threatening unforeseen outcomes, and sunny skies cannot be promised until the transiting ones move out of alignment.

"Yeah, sure, but I know he is going to be fine now that the surgery is over. Thanks again, Jan."

"I will put you on hold and then get my boss on the line for you," I said. "I am really glad things went well."

I remembered the feeling I had when I looked at the candle, and I saw the red blood in it and the great wall of bad aspects in the astrology chart of Charles' father. Then, I went back to working on a mailer I needed to get out, tossing my thoughts out of my mind and tagging them with the label of a vivid imagination.

The next day my boss stopped by my desk to get his mail.

"Remember when Charles called me yesterday?"

"Yes," I said.

"I was just talking to a couple of legislators on my way over here. Apparently, his father died," he said as he turned and walked towards his office.

My world went spiraling out of control for a couple of days, but no one around me knew it as I sorted out life, astrology, candles, Spirit, and other dimensions in my head, all while trying to make sense of how I could have seen the approaching death when no one else did.

I heard a door open from the back of the building, which instantly brought me back to my chair where I was seated in the candle shop where the class was about to start.

Malanga entered the room. Her dark eyes were captivating as she greeted everyone and then gave a brief history of her life. She grew up in the Bayous of Louisiana where swamp people practiced voodoo. Had I known this fact about her I probably would have kept my twenty-five dollars, bought a pizza, and read a book that evening. Then, I wouldn't have been exposed to all I heard that evening.

"Take your candle in your hand. If you want to attract something to you, then you point the candle towards you and stroke it in your direction with lemon juice. This action will cleanse and bless the candle. It will also attract angels. Now say your intent. In other words, what is your prayer or wish?" she concluded. "If you want to dispel something," she turned the candle away from her, "then point and stroke the candle away from you," she added.

That was simple enough, but she was leading me deeper and deeper into the dark forest that would take me off my well-lit path in life once more.

"If the moon is waxing (from new moon to full moon), then your intent, by wish or by prayer, should be to attract something. However, when the moon is waning, growing smaller from full moon to new), then your intent, by wish or by prayer, should be to dispel something."

"It is all in the wording," I mentally chuckled to myself. "If I wanted money, then I must burn the candle with the intent of attracting money when the moon is waxing. When the moon is waning, then I just need to ask to dispel poverty or financial restraints."

Selma left the room for a minute and then returned with a tray full of candles. These candles were not typical tapers. These items were wicked looking candles.

Malanga held up a wax candle that resembled a black skull.

"This skull candle is used to reverse spells," she said.

Then Malanga reached down and picked up a pink candle, causing my jaw to drop.

"This candle represents a male penis. If you want your mate to be sexually faithful, then you take a razor and prick a tiny hole into the indentation at the top of it and stick one of your pubic hairs into it. Then burn it." Then, with a twinkle and a gleam in her eyes, she added, "He will be faithful; I promise."

My eyes searched for the exit to the room. The window blinds were pulled shut so no one could see into the building. Suddenly, I felt as though I were wading in the swamps of the Bayou, searching for crocodiles I couldn't see that were going to bite me.

Malanga held up another candle. "You can see two people who are kissing in this candle. It is the lover's candle. Young women buy these to attract boyfriends," she smiled.

"Maybe I will survive this class after all," I thought.

"Next, I want to teach you about granulated garlic," she said, while holding up some granules in a jar.

"Garlic really does ward off evil spirits. If you ever feel threatened or want to dispel negative energy, use granulated garlic. All you have to do is sprinkle some along any opening to your home such as windows, doors, or even the garage door and entrances to it."

Not long after that incident, I was able to test Malanga' theory on garlic.

Back then, I lived in a condo where my Hispanic neighbor and I were feuding because of the noise his cats made while running back and forth on the ceiling of my condo.

He was furious with me for having said something about the problem, and he and his wife wouldn't speak to me for months. Not wanting our silence to continue, I went outside early one morning and sprinkled granulated garlic at the base of the stairwell he had to go down to go to the parking lot.

That day, when I was pulling my car out from the garage, I saw my neighbor motioning to me with his hand.

"Oh, crap," I thought to myself. "Is he madder than ever? Did he smell the garlic or worse yet see it?" I wondered.

I rolled the window down. He came running over to me.

"There is a man ringing your doorbell," he said.

"Thank you," I smiled back. Then, I parked my car and got out to see who was at the door. My neighbor and I spoke from that day forward.

At a different time, a neighbor of mine was frantically securing windows with a hammer and nails because someone broke into her car that was parked in her driveway the night before. I went to my kitchen cupboard and pulled down some granulated garlic that I used on steaks when I grilled them on the barbecue. I took it across the street and instructed her to sprinkle it outside around the windows and the garage door, which calmed her down.

"Thank you. Thank you," she kept saying.

Looking back, I wonder if the garlic was really warding off negative forces or just neutralizing negative thoughts from the chaos each one of us creates from our own fear.

However, if I wanted to really cleanse a house and get any negative vibrations out of it from people who had previously lived in it or just remove the negative thoughts that had piled up from chaotic times, I simply reverted back to what I learned whole studying Native American traditions, and I would burn sage to cleanse it.

Sage is an herb that grows in the desert. There are many varieties. If I wanted to use sage, then I would go to the local health food store and buy it as it came already to go in a neat little bundle. I would light the sage over an abalone shell and blow on it until red hot ambers appeared. Then, I walked from room to room wafting the smoke, paying close attention to corners of the room where energy tends to gather.

When I was cleansing negative energy from a person, I would have the sage in one hand and a beautiful long feather in the other. I would waft the smoke towards the person, moving the burning sage upwards from top to bottom and from bottom to top. It got to the point that I was so good at using sage that at the request of the Church's secretary, I once cleansed a church in Sacramento along with many homes, including one belonging to one of my neighbors who feared she had a ghost in the attic.

"Is a child blowing out a candle practicing magic or witch-craft?" I wondered. "Are people who are putting intent into candles they light casting a spell or saying a prayer?"

One of my sons, who was raised as a Baptist, once said, "You talk to dead people, Mom."

"YUK," I cringed. "I don't talk to dead people," I said to myself in disgust. "Well, I have talked to ghosts and seen them, too," my mind later reasoned. "I prefer the word, 'Spirit,' to dead people, thank you very much," I laughed inaudibly.

One thing is certain, at least in my world, it all comes from the same FORCE or source, magic, prayer, witchcraft, or near death experiences. People often use first impressions to tag everything they see as good or evil without realizing that all energy comes from the same source. There is divine order in everything. Something may appear negative, like a sickness. However, there may be a lesson to learn from the sickness. Sometimes what we learn comes from lessons we came to learn that were rooted in something we failed to learn in a past lifetime. Hasty judgment, and tags, probably sent many innocent women considered to be witches to their deaths in Salem when in reality they may have had husbands having affairs who needed their spouses out of the way.

Judgment and negative thoughts people have towards each other have caused wars and political enemies that still continue to this day.

In my heart I knew what would happen if you took the Virgin Mary you saw in a picture, let her wear the same flowing garment, but call her a Goddess, and place her in a cornfield where people gathered, wanting to be in her presence. Other people, seeing this while passing by, of a different religious persuasion, would come throwing stones at her while yelling, "WITCH," in the name of God.

Chapter 5

I sat at my desk, sorting through my mail. In a small white envelope, there was a card from an astrology client for whom I recently did a reading; she was thanking me for helping her to put to rest an old relationship, one where she continued to have feelings for the man even though they had broken up over 40 years ago. Now, she could finally move on with her life.

The "Spirit School" helped me enormously when it came to counseling my clients. Lessons I learned, often times the hard way, gave me insights I could share with my clients such as I had done with the woman who sent me the thank you card. Akar was always close by, talking in my ear, which caused me to often stop what I was saying and just quote what he wanted said.

First, I would draw up the person's astrology chart. To do the chart, I needed to know the date and time of the client's birth along with the location of where he or she was born. After I put the information into my computer, a circular wheel would appear on the monitor. The wheel was divided by twelve houses. These houses represented doorways into different aspects of a person's life, which allowed me to enter and survey the setting. One house related to the impression a person made on other people and that same house showed how he or she felt about him or herself. Other houses related to money, education, family, loved ones and children, health, while still another house related to partners -- whether it was in business or a marriage. Then, there were more houses that offered me rooms I could enter that related to inheritances, travel, philosophy and career not to mention ones that related to our friends, hospitals, seclusion and imprisonment.

The signs that appeared outside each house gave the room, or that area of their lives, its theme. For example, if Virgo was in the first house of someone's astrology chart, it meant that person could be extremely self-critical and would invest a lot of time trying to make a favorable impression on others, which was an endless worry for him or her. Yet, if I took the same sign of Virgo and put it on the second house of money, I got a completely different story. Now, the individual was worried about his or her finances all the time and fearful there wouldn't be enough money if something dreadful happened. If Virgo was on second house, it meant Leo would now be the sign governing the first house in the Zodiac belt. Whereas before, when Virgo was there and the person worried about how other people perceived him or her, the sign of Leo changed all that. Leo caused the individual to walk with pride, knowing that he or she was loved by everyone. Now, the person had an outstretched hand, eager to meet whomever he or she encountered.

Another interesting example of the signs is to take Cancer and put it on the first house. Now the person would be extremely sensitive and more reserved. If that person felt threatened, he or she would retreat into a shell much like the crab on the ocean. Put Cancer on the second house of money, and people could hoard money or feel safe and secure when they had money in the bank. If Cancer was placed on the fourth house of the home, then it was the home that made a person feel secure. Cancer on the seventh house made the person feel safest when he or she was married. Cancer on the tenth house could make the client a workaholic

The signs on the houses set the stages for the rooms of someone's life I would find myself entering in a reading. However, it was the individual planets that were the bigger-than-life characters, foretelling the circumstances the person would face. For example, Saturn would be a task master and restrict the person in whatever house in which the planet was placed. If Saturn appeared in the first house, the person was born with Darth Vader, who blocked him or her at every turn and made the person feel like he or she had to get Vader's approval before he or she accepted him or herself, if the person ever did. Saturn was also the planet of karma (lessons or the result of actions carried over from a previous lifetime). This planet brought heavy lessons or responsibilities based on the house it was in. Often times, if Saturn was in the fifth house in a woman's chart, it caused her to long for the children she couldn't bear. However, if the woman did have children, and Saturn was in her fifth house, it meant heavy responsibilities, such as one would find if he or she were raising the children alone. So, it was darned if you do and darned if you didn't have little ones.

There were nine planets in all counting the moon. Jupiter brought with it abundance and often times joy, while Mars was a driving force and sometimes the bully. Mercury was the messenger, and Venus brought love wherever it fell in the chart. But each planet did not always stand alone. That situation is when it got complicated. If Saturn was conjunct Venus, then one person could feel very committed in love, while another might not be able to feel love at all because of the heavy vibration of Saturn. When Mars was conjunct Venus in a birth chart, then the person experienced love in whatever house it fell in unless Neptune was also conjunct, which could stir deception and feelings of betrayal into the mix.

It was not easy reading an astrology chart. For me to be able to read one the way I could meant a lifetime of study and enrollment in "Spirit School," which brought with it my most important teacher, Akar. Akar's words whispered in 1 ear, and during a reading, it would literally cause cold chills and goose bumps to run down my arms and sometimes my whole body. Many gifted psychics experience the same sensation, and they call it the "Holy Spirit."

One thing I found interesting as an astrologer trying to break the code on the astrological map that would turn it into a horoscope was the difference in time from one dimension to another. It would take years before I realized that when I gazed upon a chart, the tranquil state slipped me into a different dimension and time zone. In that place, I was shown things about the client in seconds but that information would take me an entire hour to explain.

On more than one occasion, long after a reading, I received phone calls or cards from women who came to me who said I was able to predict the birth of their children within weeks of when they were born even though they were not expecting at the time.

Sometimes, the readings I did for clients involved life-threatening situations. One such case was a reading I did for a woman named Jolene.

"There is a call for you on line 2," said the receptionist in the legislator's office for whom I was working.

"This is Jan. May I help you?" I asked.

"I need to see you!" cried out the woman at the other end of the phone. "I need a reading. It is urgent," she sobbed.

"Who is this?" I questioned.

"Jolene," she replied.

"I don't do readings when I am at work," I explained.

"I have to see you. It is a matter of life and death," she insisted.

"No. I am working. I can see you after work."

"It might be too late," she said.

"It might be too late for what?"

"I might be dead. He tried to kill me. I have to see you now," she pleaded.

It was against my rules to see someone while I was at work, but Jolene sounded desperate. There was an ephemeris, a book which would show me where the planets were when she was born, which I kept in my desk drawer, but it meant I was going to have to calculate her astrology chart by hand.

"Jolene, do you remember what your ascendant or rising sign is on your astrology chart?" I asked

"No. But I have the chart you used when you did a reading a few months ago."

"It is 10:30 a.m. now. Bring the chart with you, and I will break all my rules and do a reading for you on my lunch hour," I said.

"Thank you. Thank you."

"I won't be able to tape the reading for you because I don't have a recorder here at work."

"The District Attorney's office loaned me a tape recorder. I will bring it," she said.

"Why would the DA's office loan you a tape recorder?" I asked.

"Because he confessed to other murders when he was trying to kill me," her voice was shaking.

"None of this is making any sense to me. Just come here at noon, and I'll see what I can do to help you."

"I'll be there."

When Jolene arrived, the receptionist escorted her back to my office. I could tell from the look on my coworker's face that she questioned why this person wanted to see me, especially since her wrist was wrapped in a white bandage, and she was holding a tape recorder.

Jolene would stand out when she entered a room even if she wasn't wearing a bandage. Her bleach-blonde hair that cascaded down her shoulders drew attention away from the many face lifts she had. Her waist was tiny, and she looked like a city cow girl with her white leather jacket trimmed with frills.

"Hi, Jolene," I greeted her as I stood and walked towards her. "Have a seat," I added, pointing to a chair next to my desk.

"Thank you for seeing me," she sobbed. Her hand shook when she reached down to remove a handkerchief from her purse. Then, she wiped away the tears from her red swollen eyes.

"Do you have the astrology chart I did before with you?" I asked, knowing how much work it would take for me to calculate it without the software on my computer at home.

"Yes. Here it is." She reached back into her purse and then handed me a folded piece of paper.

"Jolene, try to tell me what happened, so I can know what I am looking for when I study your astrology chart."

"There is a man I have been seeing. Together we opened a bar. He was going to finance it. I was going to fix it up and draw people to it."

"That doesn't sound threatening at all," I said with a puzzled look on my face.

"I am getting to it. He left the country to go to Spain and visit his mom. But he came back early without telling me he was coming."

"Is he Spanish?"

"Yes. He is a handsome hot-blooded Latin man, and he is extremely jealous.

"Ok. You said he came back early?"

"Oh Yes. He did. It was midnight. He used his key to come into the coach I was living in that was in back of the bar. I guess he wanted to surprise me. But he went crazy when he found me in bed with another man."

Jolene started crying. She mumbled words, but they made no sense.

"Slow down. Breathe. I need to know what I am looking for when I glance at the chart," I repeated.

"He wants to kill me," she blurted in tears. "The man I was with is dead. He shot him and then took a knife and slit my wrist," she sobbed.

"No wonder you are so frightened," I said trying to comfort her.

"Where is the man now?" I asked.

"He is locked up in jail. Someone heard a gunshot and called the police before he was able to kill me. Then, I was rushed to the hospital."

I plugged in the tape recorder that already had a fresh tape in it.

Then, I took her astrology chart which showed me where the planets were when she was born. Next, I placed several transiting planets around the outer edge of the wheel. This arrangement showed me how current planetary placements were impacting the birth chart. There before me, I saw what was making her feel threatened. I locked the moon into the aspects, so I could get a time factor as to when she really was in danger.

"The only time I see that you need to be concerned with is Tuesdays."

Jolene gasped with a surreal look on her face as her eyes studied mine.

"Tuesdays is when he is allowed to make one phone call. He calls me then, saying he lives for the day he will get out, so he can kill me before killing himself," she sobbed.

"Good. We have your most dangerous time locked in."

"What is so good about it? I am afraid to go home. I have been hiding out," she said.

"I have studied where all the planets are, and the only difficult aspects being made in the chart is on Tuesdays. It is only that day each week that the moon is making difficult aspects for you. This problem will pass when the planets move out of alignment with your birth planets. So, you don't have to hide out all the time, just Tuesdays, until this can blow over," I said, trying to reassure her.

"You don't think he will kill me?" she asked.

"Jolene, I can only see the cycles. I can't promise anything, but you are not in danger every day. I don't understand; why do they let him call you?"

"The DA's office lets him call me, so I can find out the names of the other people he has murdered in the past. He confessed to me that he was guilty of those other murders the night he slit my wrist, so that is the reason for the tape recorder. It isn't mine. It belongs to the DA's office."

"In three weeks, the planets will move on, and any threats will leave then," I added.

"Thanks so much for seeing me. I really appreciate it. I am still frightened, but you nailed the Tuesday calls that were scaring me the most. So, I feel a lot better."

She stopped the recorder that had been taping our conversation; then, she got up and left the office.

There was another time I remember when Tuesday was the key day of the week for a client that stands out over the countless readings I've done over the years.

My son was only two years old, which would mean that what I recall happened 42 years ago.

I had become friends with a man much older than me whose name was Ray. He had a double chin and a big belly, but he was a nice man and always treated me and my son special. Ray knew how hard it was for a young woman to raise a son by herself, so he always paid me for any reading I did for him and still took my son and me for rides or out to dinner.

"Hi, Jan," greeted the male voice I recognized.

"Hi, Ray," I beamed. "How are you doing today?" I asked.

"Not so good. I need to see you right away. I have an astrology chart I want you to look at."

"Sure come on over," I said, sensing the urgency in his voice.

When he arrived, I fixed him a cup of coffee; then, we sat together in my office.

"I think my wife is running around on me," he said sadly.

"What makes you think that?" I questioned.

"Jan, I own the Nationwide Detective Agency. I know these things," he said. "Here is her birth information." He handed me a torn piece of lined notepaper.

"Just give me a minute to put her birth data into the computer," I insisted.

Then, I studied where all the planets were. I could see Venus sitting in the first house of her astrology chart. "No wonder she is so beautiful," I thought to myself. Her beauty was something Ray was proud of when he showed me countless pictures he took whenever we dined out.

When Ray said he thought his wife, who was half his age, was running around on him, it gave me a clue as to on what I should focus in the chart. I was looking for aspects between Venus and Mars, which would stir her sexual desires. Sure enough, there it was. Transiting Mars was in contact with where Venus was when she was born. Now, all I had to do was figure out when the Moon made an aspect to the two planets that made her so hot to trot. The moon travels around the chart every 28 days, so I knew the moon would make an aspect and be seductive for her every seven days and that aspect would last for an entire day.

"Tuesday. Tell him, Tuesday," interrupted my guide, Akar.

"I won't say she is having an affair, Ray. But I will say, if she is having an affair it is on Tuesdays. That is when she is passionate the most," I divulged noticing the dumb founded look on his face.

"That's wrong. She can't be having an affair on Tuesdays."

"Wrong?" I asked. No one ever challenged a date I calculated in an astrology chart before now.

"She can't be having an affair then because that is when she goes to mass at the Catholic Church," he blurted. "You probably don't know this about me, Jan, but I have been Catholic all my life. I was really excited when my wife decided to join the Catholic Church a few months ago. This time, your chart is wrong. She can't be having an affair and seeing someone on the same night she goes to church."

"It's all I've got, Ray. That time is when her sexual desires are heightened the most. Maybe she is ignoring them, but it is what my calculations show," I maintained never mentioning the fact that Akar was confirming the date my eyes were shown by following the moon.

"Good. It must mean she isn't having an affair after all," he beamed. Then, he got up and left.

A few days later, I got a phone call.

"You were right." I recognized Ray's voice instantly.

"I don't understand. What was I right about?" I asked.

"I found my wife's diary. It was coded, WML; every Tuesday, it said the same thing you did," he asserted.

"What does WML mean? I thought she went to Mass on Tuesdays," I replied, confused.

"WML stands for We Made Love. She was having sex with the priest every Tuesday. I confronted her with it, and she confessed to it and broke down in tears. The next day, I drove over to the Catholic church and talked to the man who was in charge of the priest. I was so furious. The man I talked to reassured me that the priest was being sent back to Ireland because of sexual accusations made by another woman, accusations that were confirmed by their investigation. Apparently, the woman was jealous when she found out the priest was seeing someone else. That someone else was my wife."

"Wow, I would never have expected that," I replied in disbelief.

"The worst part about it is that I have been a Catholic all my life. This was my belief, my religion. She was the new kid on the block." I could hear the hurt in his voice.

Now that I think about it, there was one other reading I did for Ray, which turned out to be the last one I would ever do. As a private detective, he was often called upon to investigate some pretty big cases. One such case was when San Francisco Mayor Alioto's wife was missing.

He was my friend. At times, that friendship was both a curse and a blessing. It was a blessing because his readings that were only five dollars back in those days gave me extra money to buy things I needed for my son.It was a curse because every day I would get home from working at the State Capitol and picking up my son at day care, I would end up having Ray call me around 6:00 p.m. It was annoying because I would be tired, but I felt sorry for him. He was lonely since his wife divorced him after he caught her with the priest, and often times he was also depressed.

"I've called to say goodbye," he mumbled one evening when I picked up the receiver to the phone.

"Where are you going?" I asked, trying to sound like I cared, while I stirred some spaghetti I was making for dinner.

"I can't take it anymore. I am going to commit suicide," he confided in a barely audible voice.

Then, I did the unthinkable, something no astrologers in their right minds would do.

"Hang on for a minute, please, while I look at your astrology chart," I said. I never looked at his chart. Instead, I kept stirring the spaghetti.

"Are you still there?" I asked, picking up the receiver.

"Yes," he answered barely present.

"Ray, you can't commit suicide. I looked at your chart, and it does not say you are supposed to commit suicide."

"What?"

"You can't commit suicide until I can predict it," I teased.

Suddenly, Ray roared with laughter, which told me he was going to be okay, at least for one day or until he called me again.

"Thanks, Jan."

"Have a good evening," I chuckled with a smile, knowing I did a good deed.

However, death was lurking around Ray. It just wasn't that moment in time. Maybe, he sensed it.

A few weeks later, Ray asked me to look at another astrology chart.

"Here is the birth information you need, Jan." Ray set the piece of paper on my desk.

"She's pretty young, Ray. Are you robbing the cradle?

"No. No. Nothing like that," he quickly offered.

"She's staying with me right now. I want to go out of town with her, but I want to know what her chart looks like for taking a trip."

"That seems like a strange request. You want to know what her chart looks like in case you go on a trip with her?"

Looking at a chart to see how someone's trip is going to be if he or she is going on vacation is common, but looking at a chart to see how the planets looked in case they went on a trip seemed odd.

"I have my reasons. Just look at the two dates I have written down next to her birth data. See there at the bottom of the piece of paper?" He pointed with his finger to the dates scribbled in ink.

"I am sorry; Ray, but I don't like these dates."

"What?" he asked.

"They aren't good at all. She is upset about something, and it really looks bad. As a matter of fact, when I compare her chart to yours, I don't like the impact her planets have on you at all, especially with transiting planets making hard aspects right now. So, this isn't a good time for you to travel either. I see an attraction between the two of you. However, your Saturn is in aspect to her Saturn in both of your birth charts. This information tells me that the odds are pretty good that you both knew each other in a past lifetime and brought a lot of karma into this one."

"I feel drawn to this person. So, it doesn't surprise me if we knew each other in a past lifetime. All I know is that she was in trouble, and she is now hiding at my place," he admitted.

"Then, you don't really care what the aspects are for a trip. You are trying to see what is going on around her now?"

"Well, we might go on a trip."

"Ray, the planets are disturbing to me. Be careful with her!" I warned. "Why is she hiding out?" I asked.

"She is a prostitute. Her pimp is trying to find her. They have a child together, and she fears for her life."

"Bad JUJU, Ray," I warned again. "Leave this situation alone and do not get involved in it. I don't know how to show you what I see other than to say what I already have," I pleaded.

"She needed help. So, I helped her," he repeated like a proud hero.

"The dates you gave me look bad. No trip advised here," I repeated my warning.

"What part looks bad?" he asked even though I had asserted the same thing over and over.

"The part that looks so bad is her deep loss of a loved one. It's like a car wreck. Something happens suddenly, and she feels out of control like her whole world gets turned upside down, and it has a profound effect on her emotionally."

"I will take into consideration what you have divulged. Maybe we won't go out of town. But I am going to help her just the same," he said, getting up from the chair to leave.

Two days later, I picked up the Sacramento Bee newspaper and saw Ray's body lying on the ground of the parking lot where he lived. The caption read, "Private Investigator Murdered in Front of His Home."

My heart sank. It was the pimp. Ray was hiding the prostitute, but her pimp found her and murdered Ray. The police department didn't say who did it, but in my heart I knew. The young woman's astrology chart revealed she was going to get her heart broken, but it wasn't over Ray. It was because the father of her child was probably going to get caught and go to prison. I never would have dreamed that the loss of my heavy-set friend who dragged around a lot of emotional baggage would impact me as much as it did. When 6:00 p.m. rolled around each day, I was still expecting his call.

There was something else that I experienced with Ray's death. A rope seemed to reach out from me to him, or him to me, that didn't exist before he died. I felt him wanting to tell me he was okay. After all, he called me every evening to tell me his triumphs of the day or what the pitfalls had been. At night, I would lay awake in bed. "Where did Ray go?" I asked myself. What was really scary was nighttime was when I felt the rope pulling on me the hardest. I felt we were still connected, even more since he died than when he was alive, but I didn't know what it meant. Did he want me to join him? Was he just trying to say he was okay and wanted to check in one last time? It got that crazy. To think, this was a man with whom I was not in love, but I must have loved him.

Then, something bizarre happened. A couple of weeks after he died, I was sitting naked in my bathtub full of bubbles. The oddest thing came over me. I could feel Ray's presence. I couldn't see him, but I knew he was there. I also knew that water was a powerful conduit for psychic experiences. I wasn't scared, but I was beginning to question my sanity. Was I creating all these feelings like the connection between Ray and me, or was it all made up in my imagination? I stopped doubting what I was experiencing, however, because I knew doubt slams the psychic's portal into other dimensions SHUT.

Finally I asked, "What do you want from me? I am here, and you are... wherever you are. I can't leave this world." I paused and added, "This just makes no sense. You have to leave and go on with your journey." I tried to reason it all out in my mind. Then, I got extremely quiet.

That exact moment is when I heard Ray's voice in my mind.

"I just wanted you to know that I am okay," he assured peacefully.

Tears came to my eyes. Was the bond between he and I so powerful that it crossed dimensions?

Suddenly, the toilet seat that was sitting up for months came crashing down with a loud noise. I knew in my soul that was Ray's way of saying, "Good bye."

There was no communication from him after that time.

However, in the years that followed there were countless incidences of my seeing spirits after they crossed over or of seeing what happened to a person in a previous lifetime.

For example, one day I was attending a "message circle" at the Spirit of Grace Church. This church was not like any other that I had ever attended. Spirits were speaking to spiritually evolved people in attendance all the time. When the Sunday service was almost over, the ministers who were husband and wife would give a brief message to each person in attendance.

There was a "message circle" held at the church in the middle of the week. Only about a dozen people ever showed up. One night, I decided to attend. On this particular night, I noticed a young girl in her early twenties who was sitting in a chair across from me in the circle. She was wearing slacks and a long-sleeve blouse; she appeared fidgety at times. Nonetheless, she seemed to enjoy the messages the ministers took turns delivering, messages that they insisted were coming from Spirit.

When everyone had their individual messages and the gathering was about to come to a close, I spoke up.

"Is it okay for me to give someone here a message that I have from Spirit?" I asked. This experience was new for me, but I felt I was being asked by some mysterious force to do it.

"Of course," answered one of the ministers.

I looked over to the young woman who was wearing the slacks and began, "I see you sitting there, very calm, wearing a long skirt and a silk ruffled blouse. You are looking down, lovingly comforting a dog you are petting that is sitting on your lap. The dog is looking up at you lovingly and comforting you as well," I said softly.

Both ministers gave me a surprised look.

"Please describe the dog you see," the woman quickly pleaded.

"It is a small dog that is brown and white with long hair."

"You are describing my dog that died last week," she blurted with her eyes piercing my soul as if questioning why I was able to see what I did.

Others in the circle just looked at me in amazement.

That time wasn't the only one where I got to see the bond between an owner and a pet.

My friend Lynn loved her Golden Retriever dog, Fonsworth, so much so that she taught him to toss tidbits of food she placed on his nose into the air then catch them in his mouth. One day, Fonsworth unexpectedly became ill. The vet informed me the dog needed to be put to sleep; there was nothing more he could do for the dog. Lynn was heartbroken when her best friend, Fonsworth was put to sleep.

A few weeks after the dog died, Lynn called and asked me if I wanted to do a Native American ritual that gave thanks to all Great Spirit had provided for us. Loving a ritual and knowing many people would be celebrating the Summer Solstice; I jumped in my car and hurried over to her home in Greenhaven, a neighborhood in the Southern part of Sacramento.

I laugh now when I think about how we both thought we were such ancient and wise souls as we poured sacred blue cornmeal on her carpet forming a circle. We carefully placed a stone at the four compass points marking the four directions, North, East, South, and West. Then we laughed and danced around the room as we put ceramic fairies and other figurines around the circle, which included her "Three Sisters of Fate" statute.

"This is going to be quite a party," I beamed.

"No. Not a party," corrected Lynn in a hushed and solemn tone. It is a sacred ceremony."

"You are right. It is a ceremony."

"Not ceremony, a sacred ceremony," she corrected.
"Details, details," I laughed."

"We can't forget Fonsworth," proclaimed Lynn, racing towards a life- sized statue she bought years ago, fairly desperate to have it included in the ritual precisely because it looked so much like her dog.

"This is the most unusual ceremony I have ever done, Lynn," I commented looking around and shaking my head.

"So, it is eclectic. We've taken the best of many traditions. After all, we are just giving thanks and honoring everything for which we are thankful," she smiled.

With everything in place, I followed Lynn as she walked around the circle, lighting the candles that sat in the North, East, South, and West, using a candle I was carrying. Something strange happened when I approached the ceramic dog, however. The calm candle started wildly sparking and spitting as its flame grew higher. Then, suddenly, it stopped behaving so wildly when I moved passed the ceramic dog.

"Lynn. Did you see what just happened?" I asked.

"I know," she smiled.

"But that means Fonsworth is here!" I blurted.

"Yes, that is what I know," she commented, moving on to the next candle.

I think I went too far when it came time to saying something as the ceremony began.

"We connect with all people who are celebrating Summer Solstice and various Native American celebrations throughout the United States. We connect with birds, animals, and Great Spirit, God, Christ, and the Holy Spirit," I declared.

"I am thankful for my job," divulged Lynn, "And my friends," she added, looking towards me.

"I am thankful for my job and what I have learned about the stars, moon and heavenly planets," I burst out. "And my friends, too," I smiled looking at Lynn.

To see a dog's spirit come forth before us through a flickering candle would have been enough excitement to have from any ceremony. But that evening something else happened. It was one of those things that Lynn and I never have talked about with anyone else. We wouldn't have talked about it because no one would ever believe us.

Lynn and I were standing in her patio at midnight, while she smoked a cigarette, and I tried to stay out of the path of the smoke.

"Lynn, look!" I shouted pointing to the sky. "Do you see what I see?" I asked.

"Yes," she answered. "What in the world have we done?" "It looks like an enormous castle in the sky above your house," I muttered, studying the formation that had appeared as if out of nowhere.

"I think it looks like the Three Sisters of Fate that we used in the ceremony."

"You are right. It could be that. It is enormous," I beamed, but I was also scared. Deep in my soul, I thought we might have been playing in a ceremony that was more powerful than we thought.

That night, while driving home, I studied every inch of the sky, searching for a cloud, a touch of something that looked like cotton anywhere. Nothing! The sky was clear and filled with twinkling stars. "What did we see?" I wondered to myself. "Better yet, what energetic forces had we raised that created such a formation out of thin air?"

Chapter 6

I pulled the dark chocolate fake-fur blanket around me as I sat nestled in the corner of my leather sofa in my living room. Flickering flames danced in the fireplace while I sipped hot tea. I watched witches; monsters, skeletons and ghosts as they appeared to come alive.

Halloween was only a few days away. This year I had taken the sandstone Buddha boy, bowed in prayer, who greeted everyone when they entered my home and wrapped tiny Christmas tree lights around his head. I had placed a latex mask resembling an alien over the lights. When the lights were plugged in, it appeared as if I were seeing veins beneath the mask. His eyes lit up and studied me as I walked towards him before turning into the living room. Normally, an antique incense holder and a candle sat on a marble slab beneath the sandstone boy. In its place now was a black woven metal basket holding a small white plastic skull, a bloody hand, and a small spine bone, giving the appearance of food being offered to a monster from another galaxy.

My fireplace screen was made of chrome. Instead of it being made in three pieces that just folded open, it had two doors, which were elaborately decorated in chrome strips that unlatched and opened up in the center. These doors gave me a better view of the electric flickering logs that actually put out heat when I activated it with the remote. Since the heat wasn't as hot as real burning wood, I had ghosts and goblins climbing over the fireplace screen, which made it look like they were coming from the fire headed towards anyone sitting in the living room. To go one step further, I had a three-foot witch draped in black, complete with a broom stick, sitting on a three-foot tall round box that was covered in fake leopard skin. Printed on the skin was the face of a young leopard looking towards me.

The ambience was perfect for sipping my tea and conjuring up memories of a significant time in my life when I encountered a real ghost. It was many years ago in the home of a dear friend, Dorothy O'Malia. Dorothy and I first met when I went to her to learn how to read astrology charts. It was hard to believe I was only nineteen at the time, especially since I just turned 65 and she was now 96.

I helped Dorothy edit a book she had written in exchange for her teaching me how to draw up an astrology chart and read it. I had been studying astrology for a few years but didn't know how to draw up a chart and put the birth planets where they belonged. Prior to moving to Sacramento, I had gone to see a an astrologer in San Diego, but later I was disappointed to learn that she copied everything in the report she gave me from a book called, *A to Z Astrology*.

Despite her copying everything from a book, the report still offered a lot of insights into my life, and it made me want to know how to draw up a chart and especially how to read it. Dorothy showed me what I needed to learn. The knowledge I was learning about astrology made me feel like I was walking in Nostradamus' footsteps and seeing what the future held for individuals.

Often, Dorothy and I would stay up until the wee hours of the morning, talking about world issues and planetary alignments and what made certain politicians tick. Morning would come. We would be absolutely exhausted after an evening of accomplishing nothing tangible. A week would pass before we would find ourselves at it again.

One dark crisp and cold night like this night, many years ago, I was in Dorothy's home attending a hypnosis session she had invited me to experience. The home she lived in was a Victorian two-story home that had wooden steps leading up to the front door. The roof was sharp like a large letter A. The windows were trimmed with delicate gingerbread.

People sat in antique overstuffed chairs waiting for the hypnotist to arrive. A burning log crackled and sparked in the background

When the doorbell rang, Dorothy got up and answered it.

"Hi, Jim," she greeted him when she opened the door.

"Hi, Dorothy," responded the medium-framed man with brown hair and bangs combed back from his neatly shaved face.

"Everyone is here. We can begin when you are ready," she advised.

Jim followed her through two wooden doors that were slid open revealing everyone who was gathered to experience the regression that would take a person back into past lifetimes.

"This is Jim. He is the hypnotist that will be working with us tonight."

Everyone greeted Jim as she went around the room introducing each person to him.

She walked over to me. I was sitting in one of her antique Victorian chairs close to the fireplace. I was wearing a tight knee-high black skirt with a royal blue sweater with a plunging neckline that showed off my breast.

"This is Jan. She is the woman you will be hypnotizing first tonight."

"I am pleased to meet you, Jan," beamed Jim extending his hand to shake mine. He looked directly into my blue eyes with a smile that tattled his enthusiasm about the fact that I was his first subject for the night.

For a brief moment, I could feel a warm chemistry between us. I had anxiously waited for this moment all day. Now, I was thrilled the time had finally arrived.

Dorothy instructed Jim to sit in the seat in the middle of the room in a similar chair that was facing me. Then she walked back through the double doors to her office where a woman named Ginger was sitting in a chair next to her desk. The doorway was large enough to give them a good view of everything happening in the adjacent room that was too small for everyone to in which to fit. Ginger would be hypnotized after me.

Jim explained the regression he would be performing that night to everyone, and it was the first time I had ever heard the word "reincarnation." He was going to hypnotize me back to a time before I was born and let me see a life I once lived before this one. Then, he would do the same for Ginger.

The thought of people being able to journey back in time and see who they were in a past lifetime was exciting to me, especially since I was going to be able to meet the person I was and see where I lived and what I did in a previous life.

"Close your eyes, Jan," instructed Jim as his eyes pierced into mine.

At first, I was hesitant to close my eyes because I enjoyed the feeling I had when our eyes met.

"Now, breathe in slowly and hold it," Jim spoke softly. "Now let it out," he added a few seconds later.

I felt very relaxed.

"Now slowly breathe in deeper. Hold it to the count of ten," he paused, "Now let it out."

Jim continued to lead me through the breathing exercises a few more times. Then he said, "When I bring you out of hypnosis you will remember everything you see in this regression. Now I will count backwards. When I get to one you will feel like you are in a deep sleep."

The room was silent. The glow of the fire felt warm. I was conscious of my surroundings and how silent they had become since the hypnosis began. However, my present existence became subdued. As I fell deeper into a trance, I heard Jim say, "Three, two, one…"

"Please describe for me where you are, Jan."

I swallowed heavily before trying to speak.

"Take your time," comforted Jim. "I am here with you. Nothing is going to happen to you. Speak when you are ready."

"I am…." I muttered hesitantly, focusing on where I was.

"Take your time. Try telling me what you are wearing." coaxed Jim anxiously, waiting to see if I would respond.

"I am wearing a uniform and a hat," I answered.

"Do you know what your name is?" he asked.

"Yes. My name is Kevin," I quickly spoke up.

"Where are you?" repeated Jim, who was still trying to get his first question answered.

I was silent.

"How old are you?"

"Twenty-eight, and I am a man," I blurted, surprising even myself at my answer.

"Describe what you are seeing."

"I see a control panel. I am cramped in a small space looking out a window. It's tight. I can barely move," I explained, slightly moving my body to get more comfortable.

"Jan. Can you describe what you are seeing out the window?" asked Jim.

"I see planes chasing me and my fellow pilots. We are being attacked. I see my buddy's plane blow up in midair." My voice began to crack, and I could feel my heart racing. My body was fidgeting.

"You are okay. I am with you," said Jim. "Don't be afraid."

"What else do you see?"

The room was still. No one said a word.

"I see war planes shooting people below me. Soldiers' bodies are falling to the ground everywhere."

I didn't expect what happened next.

"Look out the window in front of you and describe what you are seeing."

"I see an enormous rock mountain. It is coming closer and closer to me," I answered with a raised voice.

"Why is the mountain coming closer?"

"I just crashed into it," I shouted. "But I left before the impact."

"What do you mean you left before the impact?"

"I lost control of my plane. Nothing was responding on the control panel no matter how hard I tried to get it to work. It was frozen. I watched the mountain getting closer and closer. Then, the plane crashed straight on into it and exploded."

I was silent for a moment.

"My body was in the plane, but I didn't get hurt," I continued. "I didn't get hurt because my soul split away the moment of impact, and I was able to see the crash and the simultaneous explosion without feeling it."

"I am going to count forward to ten. When I get to ten I want you to come forward in time, Jan, until you are back with me now."

"One, two, three, four......." Jim continued counting out loud until I heard him say, "Ten."

I opened my eyes to see Jim's eyes meeting mine with a smile. Everyone in the room was looking right at me.

"How do you feel?" he asked.

"I feel really good. Thank you for regressing me back into my past life. It explains some things in this life that I wondered about for a long time."

"Like what?" questioned Jim.

"I am deathly afraid of heights."

"No wonder you used that word 'deathly' because the crash into the mountain in midair cost you your life back then," he smiled.

I saw Dorothy walking into the room with Ginger, so I got up to give her my chair. Then, I walked into the room where she had been sitting next to Dorothy and sat down.

Dorothy came back in and sat back down at her desk. I could hear Jim counting backwards as he took Ginger deeper into a trance.

I turned to Dorothy and whispered, "That was amazing."

"Yes, I know. That is why I wanted you to be able to experience it. Reincarnation will come up in your readings for clients when you get better at reading astrology charts."

"Reincarnation shows up in a person's astrology chart?"

"Not always. But often it does," she replied.

"WOW," I whispered.

I watched Jim studying Ginger's eyes that were slightly fluttering.

"See her eyes, Jan?" asked Dorothy. "They move like that to show how deep she is in a trance."

"Oh," I responded, shaking my head affirmatively. I remembered feeling my eyes fluttering when I was hypnotized.

The fire had burned out. The room was getting dark. All that lit it was a small light sitting on Dorothy's desk in the adjacent room.

"Dorothy, this is unbelievable," I whispered, big-eyed as I heard Ginger describing a past life.

"Yes," she whispered.

Jim continued to talk to Ginger, while Dorothy and I quietly exchanged words. I was afraid of the dark, so the fire going out made me uncomfortable. A chill caused goose bumps to run down my arms. It didn't help matters that Dorothy frequently talked about having two ghosts, who she always claimed were living in her home. One was a man and the other a woman.

I focused my eyes back towards Ginger and Jim.

"Come back to the present, Ginger. Describe what you are seeing now." He coaxed.

Then, without warning, I looked deeply into the room at the corner of the ceiling. I saw a huge white swish of light swoop down and then swoop back up into the corner. Just as suddenly, it disappeared.

"I think I just saw one of your ghosts...." I teased, not finishing what I was whispering to Dorothy when I heard Ginger speak up.

"Walter has entered the room," she announced.

My jaw dropped as I looked wide-eyed at Dorothy who didn't seem to be surprised.

"It was your ghost. I saw your ghost," I said excitedly.

Dorothy just smiled, her eyes sparkling at my enthusiasm, which was like that of a small child in a candy store for the first time.

"The reason you saw the ghost in the corner of the ceiling is because the corners are powerful energy centers. They are shaped like small pyramids," she explained.

"I never noticed that they were shaped like pyramids."

"Who is Walter?" asked Jim.

"Walter is dead. He is a spirit now," she answered.

"You are going to come out of it now, Ginger," instructed Jim. "When you do you will feel refreshed. Nothing about what you have seen tonight is going to trouble you. Instead, you will have some clarity about one of your past lives. This new knowledge might even reveal how that life has affected you in this one."

Ginger was dry-eyed now and breathing normally, less agitated, more at peace.

COMMUNICATING WITH THE FOURTH DIMENSION

"I am going to count forward. When I say ten, you will slowly open your eyes and come out of the trance."

"One, two, three, four, five .... You are slowly coming out of a deep sleep now. Six, seven, eight.... Now you will awake feeling refreshed and wide awake. Nine and ten. Come out now," instructed Jim.

Ginger opened her eyes and looked up at Jim without noticing all the eyes in the room glued on her.

"I have never experienced anything like this before," she spoke softly, trying to process everything that had happened in her mind.

"Was there anything about the past life you visited that explains feelings you might have in this life?" asked Jim.

"Yes. Since I was buried alive in that lifetime, but no one knew I was still alive, but in a comma, I have insomnia," she confided. "It's really bad. I just can't go to sleep. I guess it is because I am afraid I won't wake up if I do, or someone will bury me alive and think I am dead," she surmised.

It was getting late. Everyone present thanked Dorothy as they left, especially Ginger.

"Thanks, for coming, Jim. I appreciate it," said Dorothy graciously.

"It was a great session. I am glad I was able to do it," he replied.

After Dorothy closed the door, she came back into her office where we sat talking for a while. I had to know more about reincarnation and astrology.

However, the hour was late, and I had to leave without getting the answers that would actually take a lifetime to get. But she did walk me to my car.

"Goodnight, Dorothy," I said, giving her a hug. "And thanks for walking me to my car. I am so frightened of the dark."

"Perhaps sometime we can explore what made you afraid of the dark in a past lifetime," she laughed, returning my hug.

She turned and walked back up the steps leading to her home, while I waited to make sure she was safe before driving off.

Chapter 7

I was busy cleaning the tinted picture window in my living room when I noticed the UPS delivery man parking his truck in front of my house.

"It's finally here," I beamed, signing for the huge brown box the young man was holding.

"Is it something special?" he asked, handing me the package.

"There is a drum in it," I responded, embracing the box with both arms.

"I wouldn't have expected that answer," he chuckled as he turned and walked away.

Two weeks had passed since I first sat down at my computer and began searching for a drum on, Ebay, my favorite internet auction site. Akar was egging me on -- not with words - just a feeling that seemed to rise up from my soul.

My eyes scanned picture after picture of drums listed for sale on that site. Normally, I could just let something I wanted cross my mind and then mentally I would be shown what store in town had it on sale. All my friends knew this strange ability of mine and teased me by saying, "Janice has shopping guides."

This time it was different. I didn't have a clue what Akar wanted me to find. All I knew is I would see it listed on Ebay. The drums appearing on the pages ranged from blue-glittered musical sets with cymbals used in a rock band to Djembe hand drums with hand-painted or carved artwork on their hides. Several were Native American drums in every size and shape.

Suddenly, my eyes were fixed on the drum that I knew Akar wanted me to buy, and my heart pounded as loud as it could.

Normally, I was somewhat conservative when it came to spending money, but when Spirit offered me something that had strings connecting it to my heart; money was no longer an issue.

The caption read, "Wooden Hand-Carved African Drum – Lizard Design," and right away I knew this item was no ordinary drum. It stood two-foot tall with enormous carved lizards that were wrapping their bodies around it. I counted six legs on each lizard. World Treasurers Antiques, which was located in New York, listed the item at $199 with the words, "buy it now," proudly displayed on the site, meaning I could agree to pay that amount without having to bid against other shoppers making offers on it, which is exactly what I did.

While I waited for the drum to arrive, I contacted the seller to learn more. A woman named Kathy responded to my emails by saying that she wasn't the owner of the store. The owner had traveled to Africa, picked it out personally, and then brought it back to the United States to sell in his antique store. She went on to say they sold many of their items on Ebay.

From studying the picture of the drum, I was able to determine that it was probably a Kpanlogo Peg drum from the Ivory Coast of West Africa. This realization amazed me because I knew I had once lived in Africa in a past lifetime. Now I would own something that actually came from Africa. Maybe this drum had been used in a ceremony, and maybe I had been both the maker of the drum and the drummer.

My thoughts came back the task at hand; I began to open the box with a sharp paring knife I found in my kitchen drawer. Numerous layers of newsprint were wrapped around the drum to protect it from shipping damage as it made its long journey from Africa to my home.

"Look at the enormous lizards," I shouted at the silence that filled my home. I knew lizard was often used in some societies as a totem to represent clairvoyance and the dream world.

"Lizard represents being able to see beyond the physical world into other dimensions," said Akar unexpectedly. "It feels things in the vibration of the ground on which it walks, and it acutely hears things humans can't."

"Sounds a lot like me in my world," I laughed to myself. Suddenly, I was starting to know why Akar wanted me to have this totem.

"Hmm. Now, lizard belongs to the element of fire, and without fire we couldn't manifest our dreams. It can teach us powerful spiritual lessons and bring us home," I thought to myself as I realized that for now, home was here in Sacramento, California.

"Obviously, the drum isn't new, so it would have been carved many years ago by an African living in the country where I once lived in a past lifetime," I continued to ruminate. "If there is something to destiny, and I believe there is, then perhaps the drum had been carved especially for me, and it traveled over land and sea to find me now on the other side of the world. If such abstract thoughts can be true, then maybe my imagination can stretch a bit further, and I can even say that this was once my drum, and I was the one who carved it to begin with."

I laughed at my thoughts; nonetheless, my fingers couldn't help but touch the deeply carved wood almost reverently as I studied the enormous lizards crawling up the drum. I turned it round and round, admiring the craftsmanship of my newly acquired masterpiece.

Eight wooden pegs stuck out about three inches down from the top of the drum and formed a circle around it. These pegs pierced into animal hide that had been tightly placed over the drum and then folded up again. Four rows of heavy twine secured the hide and pegs.

When I turned the drum upside down to look inside it, I could see the other half of the pegs. Each peg appeared to have been put into an enormous pencil sharpener and shaved down to a dangerously fine point. There was a frightening feeling of something tribal lurking inside the drum. I felt like I was falling down into a dark cave where a Banshee was going to fly towards my face any minute and scare the living daylights out of me. The stain of the drum made it look like it had been dipped in dark roasted coffee.

A moment later, chills ran up my arms when I watched my dog Max freak out when he first saw the drum sitting on the floor near my fireplace.

"Ruff, Ruff, Ruff," he barked profusely.

No, Max," I scolded.

"Ruff, Ruff, Ruff," he persisted with legs planted firmly on the carpet protruding his chest in a threatening stance.

About then, Simba, my 22-pound orange and white cat, came strolling into the room. It was always Simba's job to check out anything that had been changed in the house, and the living room was a particularly sensitive spot for that cat.

Max saw Simba and wanted to play a game the two of them always played, a game I called, "Dog Chases the Lion." I laughed as I watched the little white dog chase Simba down the hall past the jungle scene I had painted on its walls.

I sat on the floor, once again admiring the drum, while my thoughts wandered as I tried to figure out other reasons I was supposed to have this magnificent hand-carved beauty. Within seconds, Akar answered my unspoken questions.

"You needed the drum because each beat sounds like it is echoing through the jungle. Right now, you are drawn to the life your soul recalls in Africa because a part of you remembers your deeply rooted tribal traditions. They were rooted and grounded right into the Earth. Mother Earth is healing and comforting. This drum can heal you when you are sick or unsettled."

My hand tapped the top of the drum. The sound echoed and drew my heart into the middle of the jungle -- just like my Spirit guide, Akar, said.

Looking back now, I cannot help but wonder how Akar knew I was going to need something to ground me. At the time, I didn't have a clue I would soon face one of the greatest tests in my life. Before I knew what hit me, I would feel as though someone were squeezing my heart as hard as he or she could, leaving me with pain that would be excruciating, so much so, that I questioned whether I could even bear it. Akar, was right. I would need my roots, my tribe and anything else that grounded me. In the meantime, I just innocently followed the path I was on and created my African art -- totally oblivious to what lurked on the road ahead of me.

One such piece of art that I created at the time was the African mural that hung in four equal sized panels on the wall in my dining room.

I recalled how the mural came about. It was close to Christmas time, and I was attending a Unity Church service here in Sacramento, one that had a popular African-American minister with a large following. In front of the podium where the handsome minister stood wearing an expensive three-piece suit and polished black shoes was an abstract picture. This picture was not like any picture I had ever seen. Inside the frame were bits of burlap fabric that had designs painted on them. Some of the designs looked like spirals, while others looked like triangles. I had also glued sticks, beads, and sea shells throughout the piece I later made. My eyes were mesmerized on the artwork, and I knew it wasn't because of what I was looking at as much as it was the energy I was feeling from the person who created it.

"Today, we are celebrating an African-American holiday with which many of you may not be familiar. It is called Kwanzaa. The art piece you are looking at beneath the podium was created by a member of our congregation," the minister explained.

The church choir sang, and members of the congregation clapped their hands as their bodies swayed to the music with a Congo beat.

I never understood all the principles of the Kwanzaa but knew it had to something to do with African reflection and communication that came from the heart. I also knew I wanted to own such a piece, and the only way I would be able to have it was to make it myself.

That day, I left the church, feeling as if I were on the most important mission of my life. I stopped by a fabric store and bought several yards of burlap. I found animal prints that felt soft like fur representing different animals I would find in the jungle like a lion and a zebra. I had no vision of what I was doing, but my heart pounded with enthusiasm as I followed Akar's lead and had the different pieces cut in one yard lengths.

When midnight came, I found myself in front of my computer, going online and scanning Ebay for anything I could find that was African, i.e., decorative beads and seashells. Then I bid on them. I found hand-carved wooden animals that were carved by a monk many years ago, a monk who lived in Africa and who later brought them to the United States. I immediately placed a bid on them. Next, I found the claw of a real lion that once lived in Ethiopia, and I placed a ridiculously high bid on it to secure my winning the item. I not only won the claw, but I also won the hand-carved wooden animals as well.

Once all the items arrived, I spread the four panels that were decorated with Asian dancers and probably worth a fortune on my dining room table. The value of the panels didn't matter to me because I had bought them at a thrift store for a good price. I would use the panels to create my African art even thought I didn't really know what I was creating. Glue guns, staple guns, a pair of scissors, and a needle and thread were my tools.

In my heart, I really believe Akar was guiding my hands. Swiftly, animals that stretched their bodies and heads from one panel over to the next came to life. I mounted beads, and I cut up an African doll someone had given me, a doll that had been made by children in Africa, which really scared me. I didn't want to ruin the doll, but I needed the vibration of where it came from on my mural.

Hours passed, my hands flew, the staple gun clicked, and the glue gun burned my fingers over and over. Akar had advised to keep the intent of protection in my heart as I created the enormous mural that would span many feet across my dining room wall. So, over and over the words, "Protection, protection, protection, peace for me in my new home," swirled in my mind as I worked on what I was creating, while listening to jungle drum music beating out their rhythms as they played on my stereo. I didn't feel as if I were in danger from anything, but then again I didn't understand the significance of what I was doing. I did feel the enthusiasm, an adrenaline rush running through my body, and finally, I felt in awe as I stood back and saw what I, or Akar and I, had created.

Looking back to when I created the mural, I realize that I didn't need protection from an intruder that was going to hit me over the head and rob me. I needed it from the brutal test life eventually delivered to me.

It came far sooner than I could have ever suspected. My heart was in excruciating pain. I was alone entrapped in my very own dark inner jungle of fear. The principals of the peaceful path I once walked on, that took years to learn, were gone. Tears would fall from my eyes and sniffling would jerk me back to reality when I tried to meditate and find my peaceful place.

The painful test came right after Christmas when all the New Year's celebrations had quieted down. It was then that I received news that my youngest son, Jon, had been rushed to the hospital. The days that passed revealed he had an inoperable brain tumor that may have been growing for 30 years, which meant it had been growing inside of him since he was ten years old.

The news was too heavy of a cross for any mother to drag. Only six years had passed since the same month of January brought news of my son, Jeff, and his unexpected death. This latest crisis came at the same time I was having radiation treatments for breast cancer. To even make matters worse, and to cause a few more tears to flow, my eldest son, William, had been successfully struggling with Multiple Sclerosis for years. The odds were stacked against me; it was possible that I was going to lose all my sons, whom I dearly loved, in my lifetime.

African murals made of fabric or painted on the walls of my hall made sense now. I longed for my tribal roots, safety, and Mother Nature to embrace me. I just didn't know at the time that all of these future events would soon come into existence.

I walked over to the sink in the kitchen to pour a glass of water from the faucet. A happier mood fell over me when I glanced at my drum, sitting in all its glory and covered with powerful lizards that sometimes looked like salamanders. The fact that the drum had just arrived before all of the trouble would begin was unknown to me. At the moment, I was thrilled because it had arrived in time for me to show my friend, Michael Bayard, at his drumming healing circle, an event I was going to attend the next day. I didn't know that multiple crises lurked just around the corner. All I knew was that I had accomplished something that my guide, Akar, had instructed me to do, and I was thrilled with my own artistic expression and how well my project had turned out.

Chapter 8

Michael Bayard is a well-known Master Percussionist and sound healer. When the next evening came, I arrived early, so I could sit in the front row, a stone's throw away from the enormous mother drum Michael would be beating.

A buzzing noise echoed throughout the room. It was really just the sound of several people talking all at once, as they entered the room and found a seat. I counted approximately 126 people before I lost track because my eyes turned from the door to a grass hut that stood to the left of the stage. Beautiful paintings, artifacts, lights of various colors, and a picture projected on the front wall gave ambience to the setting.

The green flyer I was handed at the door told me that tonight the production's theme was: "*The African Shamanic Experience.*" The stage had been set to resemble a tribal village on the savannah plains in the heart of Africa which explained the grass hut I had seen.

Six-thirty finally arrived. Michael walked to the microphone in front of the crowd.

"Welcome, to Unity's Drumming and Music Medicine Circle," he smiled. "Tonight we have an exciting evening planned. You'll experience a journey to Africa."

Michael took his seat behind his enormous tribal mother drum that sat on wooden frame specifically designed to tilt the drum towards him. A loud beat of the drum from Michael silenced any talking, and all eyes turned to him. The rhythm of the sound was firm and steady. He nodded his head and pointed at the audience with his drumming stick, inviting them to join in.

The room was magical; hearts were joined with smiles, and bright eyes passing from one person to another. Eventually, a dancer came out wearing a native African costume that looked like it was made from long dried leaves. The head dress was also made from the same leaves, and it covered the dancer's face, except for two bright coal black eyes that felt like they were piercing my soul, when they looked my way. Next, the thundering resonance of a didgeridoo echoed throughout the room.

"Now, I am going to take you on a shamanic journey," announced Michael.

I could hear the steady beat on the drum that resembled a heartbeat to me. At times the pace increased. It was such times as this one that I was able to connect to other lifetimes, the fourth dimension, and see what our spirit guides really do when we our gathered with others and preoccupied with what we see visually in front of us.

As I sat in the audience, I began to recall another evening when I had been sitting in the same room and attending one of Michael's elaborate productions. During the shamanic journeying portion of the program, I found myself taken to a different dimension.

At that earlier time, major fires were burning out of control in Southern California. I sat quietly in the crowd, listening to the beat of the drum, while people hummed the musical notes that Michael instructed them to hum. Unbidden, a vision appeared before me, one that I can still see to this day. Instead of sitting in the dimly lit room, we had formed a line and were standing along the edge of our Earthly existences. We all looked upwards, and I heard us singing in tune with the harmonious music produced by the movement of celestial bodies known as the "music of the spheres." The sound was heavenly. Akar whispered to me that we were healing the Earth.

We thought we had all gathered that night to hear Michael, but I was being told by my Spirit guide that we were brought together by Spirit, so we could collectively heal the Earth even though we didn't know that is what we were doing.

On a different occasion, when the subject of the program was Egypt, I remember hearing Michael strike an enormous gong that created the sound of a fluttering bird taking flight. In that brief second, I saw Michael, living in Egypt in a past life. Later, when I emailed him what I had seen that night, he surprised me with a return email that revealed he had the exact same vision of living in Egypt when he struck the gong as I did at the very same moment as I had my vision.

But none of the visions taking me to other dimensions were as profound as the one that happened during Michael's shamanic drumming when we were taken by the theme and the beat of his drumming trip that magically transported the entire crowd to a tribal village on the savannah plains in the heart of Africa during his program on the African Shamanic Experience.

The room was dark, and pictures representing different scenes changed one by one. For me, these scenes were over-laying what I was being shown. People looked up at one thing, while my eyes saw what they did but they were simultaneously seeing something completely different than mere images projected on a screen.

Ten days prior to that evening, Brazil had the deadliest natural disaster in history. Five-hundred-and-eleven people had died, and the numbers kept climbing. The deaths were caused by unexpected flash floods and mudslides triggered by torrential rains. Hundreds of people were missing.

During the shamanic drumming, Michael projected a picture of rocks lying beneath clear water along a shore on the wall. When my mind saw the rocks in the water, I instantly felt myself slipping into a trance of sorts, and suddenly the round rocks of varying shapes were hundreds of heads that all looked different. As I went deeper, the heads became skulls. I sensed confusion and lost souls hovering from the Brazilian disaster.

"Michael's music, and everyone's drumming has been releasing the spirits that were trapped thousands of miles away," explained Akar. "The audience thinks they came to hear the music and share the experience, which they did. But their guides brought them here to help the lost souls in Brazil through vibrational healing coming from music," he added, leaving me speechless for a moment.

When the program concluded, I walked up to Michael.

"Hi, Michael," I smiled.

"Hi!" he smiled back, happy to see me.

"I brought the carved drum that comes from the Ivory Coast of West Africa that I was telling you about in one of my emails," I said, handing him the drum.

"This is really nice," he remarked studying it. Then, he struck it with his hand. "It needs to be tightened up."

"How do I do that?" I asked.

"Put a cloth over it to protect it. Then put a heating pad on it. That will tighten it," he assured me with a twinkle in his eyes.

"Thanks. Great job tonight," I added, knowing in my heart that he probably didn't know that his music was traveling to other realms and doing healing work with the support of the people in attendance along with their guides on a scale that was hard to imagine.

"Thanks," he smiled, turning to greet some people approaching him.

When I got home that night from the drumming circle, I sat on the floor by the drum, gazing at the lizards wanting to come alive.

As much as I longed to know what the carver who created it looked like, I also hungered from the depth of my soul to remember Africa.

I tapped the hide with my hand a couple of times, and the sounds of the drum's voice took my mind to Africa where I saw myself as a dark-skinned young boy, who was running barefoot as fast as he could through the jungle, as free as the wind.

My thoughts returned to the lizards. I wanted to know more. "What did the tree once look like that from which my drum was carved? What animal sacrificed its hide, perhaps unwillingly, so it could be draped over the top of the drum, allowing it to echo such a beautiful sound?" I had so many questions.

"No, I didn't just buy a drum," I thought to myself. "I bought the spirit essence of the carver, tree, and animal of which it was comprised not to mention all the people who once beat it during a special ceremony. Maybe one of the drummers was related to me in another lifetime. Maybe that drummer was me.

I went to bed early that night. Lucia, one of my dearest friends, was coming over for a late birthday celebration. Akar had advised me to leave the day open, which meant I should get plenty of rest if I was going to be a part of another one of his adventures.

Chapter 9

"Ruff, Ruff, Ruff," barked Max as he leaped down from the top of the brown leather sofa that sat beneath a huge picture window in the living room. It was his favorite look-out post.

He ran to the front door and twirled in circles as if chasing his tail. Then, he grabbed his favorite bright pink teddy bear and waited for me to open the door, so he could give his gift it to Lucia.

"Hi, Lucia," I greeted her, noticing how pretty she looked with her long blonde hair and bright blue eyes. "Come on in."

"Hi, Max," she said, reaching down with both hands to pick up him up. Then, she walked into the living room.

Lucia loved Max. It was obviously mutual.

I gave her a hug, and she hugged me back. We had known each other for many years.

"Happy Birthday," she beamed, handing me a small brown bag with handles made of twine that was stuffed with brightly colored yellow and green paper.

"You didn't need to bring me a present since you are taking me to lunch, and we are spending the day together," I said.

"I know. It's not much," she responded as she watched me pull out a large purple bottle of shower gel that came with a large soft white ball of netting for scrubbing your skin.

"Thanks, Lucia," I smiled. "Even though you didn't need to bring me something, I am glad you did."

"Glad you like it," she responded.

"I know we were planning on going to the art show at the Convention Center today, but I am getting strange vibes on that," I said.

"It seemed odd you wanted to go because it is strictly an art show. There won't be crafts there," she offered. "But we can do whatever you want. It's your birthday."

"Are you up for a short trip out of town?" I asked. "I'll drive."

"What did you have in mind?"

My mind scanned all areas around Sacramento.

"Do you remember the glass chimes you bought me in Auburn for my birthday years ago?" I asked.

"Yes," she responded with a curious look in her eyes.

"Later, you took me to the store where you bought them. I remember going into metaphysical and art stores. A few months ago, I tried to find my way back to those shops, but nothing was familiar."

"The place I bought the wind chimes from closed. It was in Historic Auburn. However, there are metaphysical stores in Old Auburn," she explained.

"Historic Auburn? Old Auburn? I said, confused.

"The owner of the metaphysical store, Planet Earth Rising in Folsom, has a sister running a store in Historic Auburn that is called The Quiet Path.

"I didn't know that. Let's go," I grabbed my purse, which was sitting on the counter and reached into it for my car keys.

"Sure." Lucia put Max down and got up from where she was sitting on the sofa and followed me out of the house.

Max was on top of the sofa, watching as we pulled out of the drive way. His eyes looked sad as if he felt heartbroken we were leaving.

Lucia and I got each other caught up on what was happening in each of our lives as we drove down Highway 80 headed for Auburn.

Fall displayed the strokes of Mother Nature's art brushes. The countryside was sprinkled with breathtaking maple trees, bearing bright red leaves with patches of yellow ones. Sometimes the leaves were a blend of pink, red, and yellow and were so transparent that it felt like I could reach right through the leaves without ever touching them.

I parked the car on a steep slope across the street from the metaphysical shop. I could see crystals, statuary, and figurines in the window with a sign on the white building that said, The Quiet Path.

"Hello," an elderly gray-haired woman with a few strands of red hair left over from younger years greeted us. Her fair skin revealed age spots.

"Hi!" I spoke up. "I love what you have done with your shop," I said, admiring several quartz crystal clusters.

"Oh, thank you," responded the frail woman as she rummaged through things around her cash register, searching for something she misplaced.

To my right, I could see beautiful cotton clothing with long purple skirts and matching long purple jackets with contrasting white bursts of lines and circles in the print that resembled abstract flowers.

A glass case displayed shelves of jewelry. There were some silver crosses in different sizes. A couple of the quartz crystal pendants had seven tiny stones in different colors mounted down the front of them representing different chakras (energy centers in the body).

Peaking around a corner was a gorgeous three-foot tall statue of swimming dolphins mounted in marble. I would have bought it in a heartbeat if the tag didn't say $340.00.

On a shelf in the opposite corner of the room from where I was standing, I spotted a Zen garden that seemed to be calling out to me. I walked towards it, while Lucia roamed into one of the back rooms.

An oval black pottery dish with a one-inch lip was filled with fine white sand that resembled white flour. An agate slab with tiny crystals in it held a tiny mud man who was smoking a white pipe. Flagstone pieces were scattered about resembling mountains. Strange things like a tiny star fish and small metal trees near a mounted crystal sphere were also in the dish. It was way too cluttered for a Zen garden, but I could feel the energy of the person who placed the pieces in the sand, and something told me it wasn't the woman keeping the store.

I had been searching for a Zen sand garden on Ebay's online auction for weeks but couldn't find one I liked. If I did see one I liked, then thoughts of my huge 22-pound orange-and-white cat, Simba, always blocked me from bidding on it.

When I was in Missouri years before and planning my move back to California, I tried to figure out a way to carry Simba in a cage in the car with me. I found a small box and filled it up with sand. When I put it in front of Simba, he would take his paws and throw sand all over the floor as if his purpose in life was to find sand and dig in it.

Simba happily emptying the sand from my Zen Garden on my glass-topped dolphin coffee table was only one of my fears. What if he thought my Zen Garden was a place to deposit his own brown rocks instead of keeping them in his litter pan? The wooden rake that came with the set was supposed to be used to quietly rake the sand around the rocks as one slipped deep into thought; it wasn't meant to rake out Simba's poop. I didn't dare take a chance and buy any of them, yet I was drawn to this one.

"If I were to buy your Zen Garden that you have displayed here, would the pieces displayed in the sand come with it?" I asked, turning to the woman who was the owner.

"They don't come with it, but if you see a piece you like, I could include it," she advised, walking towards me to studying the value of what was scattered on the sand.

"I was interested in the Zen Garden the way it is set up already," I replied.

"Well," she hedged, looking at the agate crystal slab holding the mud man. "I guess I could let you have it with everything in it if that is what you want," she replied hesitantly.

"Let me give it some thought. I have a cat, Simba, and I am not sure if he will leave it alone or not," I laughed.

"You wouldn't want your cat thinking it was a sandbox," she chuckled.

"I know. My friend and I want to check out a few more shops around town. If I decide to get it, I will come back," I said before turning to walk to the front door where Lucia was waiting for me.

"Remember, I close at 5:00 p.m.," cautioned the old woman.

"I am really getting hungry. Are you getting hungry, Lucia?" I asked as I walked out of the shop.

"I could use some food about now," she answered. "There is a Goodwill thrift store close by. You could buy a dish for your Zen Garden there and then go to Michael's craft store and buy the white sand. You would save yourself a ton of money if you made your own Zen Garden," she added.

"Believe me, I am the queen of saving money, and I know that I could. Not sure why, but I am drawn to the one in the store. BUT, if there is a Goodwill close I would love to check it out since we are already here."

We both got into the car and drove through town.

"There's an In-and-Out Burger over there," pointed Lucia to the fast food place right of us, "Or we could go to Chevy's and have Mexican food. Lunch is on me for your birthday."

"In-and-Out Burger sounds fine," I answered, making a right-hand turn that led me up a hill to their parking lot.

After lunch, we drove a couple of miles to the Goodwill thrift store. Inside, we searched for inexpensive treasures that were once expensive. A baby doll caught my eye. It was about eight inches long and wore pink pajamas. It had 99 cents written on its forehead in red. I spit on the tip of my finger to see if I could rub off a tiny bit of the lettering to make sure someone hadn't used permanent ink. The ink rubbed off, right onto my index finger, but it wouldn't come off my skin. There was a paper tag on the doll attached with tape on its leg.

"This once belonged to my grandmother's grandmother in the 1800's. My son owned this fan after that," the tag read.

"Wow," I thought to myself. At first, I thought the doll was from the 1800's. She was a vintage doll, but it was a fan someone was referring to on the piece of paper. I quickly scanned the bin I had pulled the doll out of but didn't see any fan.

"Someone is going to find a real treasure," I thought to myself. "It's too bad they won't have the history that goes with it.

"Mama," the baby doll said when I squeezed her belly too tight.

"Daddy," it cried when I squeezed it again.

"Aw choo," echoed the baby on the third squeeze.

"A baby with allergies," I laughed to myself out loud.

"This is wood. It would work for the sand of your Zen Garden," hinted Lucia walking up from behind me.

"That is a nice find. But I might not even make one," I said, putting the doll into my basket. Simba, was too unpredictable, and I still wasn't convinced that it was going to be okay to have a Zen Garden on my coffee table.

"Look here, Jan," cried out Lucia with excitement. "It's a knitting loom to make scarves. The price tag on it from Wal-Mart says $24 but here they are selling it for only $4. I am going to buy it," she said, putting it in my cart.

"I am done. Are you ready to go?" I asked.

"Sure am," she smiled.

We paid for our treasures. The Zen Garden was still on my mind.

"Do you want to go to Grass Valley and check out the Altar Show? I think it is today," said Lucia walking toward the car.

"Altar Show?" I questioned her with a puzzled look on my face.

"Let me see, first," she remarked pulling out her cell phone. "Yep, it's today."

"What is today? I have never heard of an altar show before," I said, feeling a bit frustrated that I she knew something I did not.

"Every year there is an annual altar show held at the Nevada County Fairgrounds in Grass Valley. They display altars that are made for honoring the dead, paying tribute to life, or promoting a cause. The energy is awesome," she explained.

"You have got to be kidding me?" I blurted in disbelief. "You have been to it before?"

"Yes," she answered.

"Of course, I want to go. I would love to go. BUT could you drive for a while?" I asked.

"Hand me the keys," she replied.

"I have a GPS system. I will have it look up the fairgrounds," I said, plugging it into the system.

"Great."

"The GPS is saying we will be there in 30 minutes. I didn't realize it was so close. I am surprised I never knew about the a\Altar Show before now."

"You will love it. It will make celebrating your birthday even more special," said Lucia.

"Eighteen months ago, I was traveling down this same road on my way to Ananda Village in Nevada City," I said, admiring the landscape, which was filled with trees that were busy showing off their brightly colored leaves. My favorites were the orange maples until we traveled a few miles further down the road, and I saw tall pine trees with patches of white snow on them.

"Nevada City isn't far from where we are going," explained Lucia.

"Did I ever tell you what happened to me when I went to Nevada City last year? I will never forget it. It had Akar's signature on it much the same as our trip today," I offered.

"No. You never did," commented Lucia, keeping her eyes on the winding road ahead.

"Casey, a friend of mine was coming to visit me from out of state. I was trying to figure out somewhere we could go while she was in town that would be different. I was sitting at my computer checking out Yosemite. It was a place I knew neither of us had ever been to. But when I looked it up, I saw it was closed because of snow storms they had been having. It was then that I heard Akar say, 'Ananda Village,' which really surprised me."

"Your Spirit guide still talks to you?" Lucia smiled.

"Yes. But something unusual happened earlier that day. I needed to go to the supermarket. I drove away from my home and turned onto a busy street that runs behind my house. I had traveled down this same road every week for over a year -- never noticing a sign I saw that day. It read, 'Open Daily Meditation,' and it was hanging around an iron gate near the front of the door. In front of the building, I read a large sign with the letters printed on it, 'Ananda.' I never knew Ananda was in Sacramento. Here it was a couple of stop lights down from where I live. Now, hours later, Akar was saying, 'Go to Ananda Village.' What's ironic is that going to Ananda Village had been my dream for 45 years," I explained.

"You never mentioned wanting to go to Ananda Village in all the years I have known you, Jan."

"My spiritual journey got a jump start when I read Swami Paramahansa Yogananda's book, *Autobiography of a Yogi,* when I was only 19. I always thought for some reason that Ananda Village was in the town of Lake Tahoe. But, when Akar mentioned it, I checked out their website and noticed that Ananda Village was in Nevada City."

"It is interesting that you never saw the sign by your home before that day," acknowledged Lucia.

"There is even more that is amazing. First of all, when Casey and I went to Ananda Village, we arrived in time for their Sunday morning service. It turns out they were celebrating Paramahansa Yogananda's Mahasamadhi.

"What did you say?"

"Mahasamadhi. It means it was the final conscious exit from this world for Paramahansa Yogananda, and they were celebrating his passing," I explained. "We stayed for a delicious buffet of vegetarian Indian food that was prepared by a man who owned a Mexican restaurant in Nevada City."

"Sounds yummy," commented Lucia.

"A couple sitting at our table learned this was the first time we had been to the village. The woman motioned to a gentleman, who was sitting across the room to come to our table. Then, she asked him if he would show us around after lunch since the grounds of Ananda Village was enormous. He agreed.

"That was nice ... to have a guide," said Lucia. "The GPS says we are only ten minutes away from Grass Valley now."

"Something else happened while we were there. It still boggles my mind, and that incident is what I have been leading up to tell you."

"What happened?"

"Casey was driving down a dirt road, keeping just enough distance from the guide in front of us to avoid the dust that was flying in the air from the back wheels of his pickup. That is when I heard Akar."

Lucia smiled as I continued my tale.

"'Ask the guide about the fire,' coaxed Akar softly but firm," I continued. "In unison with Akar's words, I looked to my right at a clearing and saw a massive fire."

"What fire?" asked Lucia.

"I didn't know either, Lucia. I remember the guide told us that he only had enough time to take us to the museum because he had some errands to do in town. We followed him into a quaint wooden building that was a gift shop. A pleasant elderly woman looked up from what she was knitting. She greeted us and told us to enjoy the museum. We followed as the guide walked through the gift shop into the museum attached to it."

Lucia grinned as if she knew what was coming next.

"In the museum, I saw a room lined with enormous wooden glass cabinet cases that contained treasured items of things that once belonged to Yogananda. I saw a copper bowl that he would have once held in his hands and some of the clothes he would have worn. I could feel his presence as I walked along the cases, studying old pictures of him and his family and some of the places his journeys had taken him," I explained.

Lucia nodded her head.

"'I am sorry I am so rushed today. But my business in town was planned long before today, or I would stay and try to show you more while you are here,' said our guide," I further explained to Lucia.

She smiled, and I continued the story.

"'It is quite alright,' I responded. 'We both appreciate you taking the time to bring us here and show us the museum.'"

I looked at Lucia and explained that Casey and I said goodbye to the old woman on our way out.

Lucia kept listening.

"'Have a nice day and come back some time when you can stay longer,' the woman said, giving us a lovely smile as we were leaving," I continued. "Our guide led the way up a small hill to where our car was parked next to his pick-up truck."

Lucia raised her eyebrows as I went on to say what happened next.

"Well, Lucia, you can imagine my surprise when Akar piped up and said, 'Ask about the fire.' Of course, I did. 'Sir,' I said standing by my car. 'Spirit keeps asking me to ask you about a fire I saw in a clearing on our way up here. Do you know anything about a fire?' Before he had a chance to answer, I described exactly where the fire was, Lucia," I continued.

"Amazing," commented Lucia studying the exit signs on the road ahead.

'Yes there was a fire,' acknowledged the tour guide looking straight in my eyes, knowing whatever my source was – it was right on. 'It was back in the 70's when the community was just getting started. Many buildings burned and it happened in the clearing you described,' he commented.'"

"Wow," said Lucia looking towards me in awe.

"As Casey drove us back out of the property, I studied the trees. There were no burnt leaves, no charcoal on the ground or blackened cleanings. Yet, I saw it all as if it was happening while we were there."

"You know what that meant don't you?" asked Lucia.

"Yes, the energy of what happened never left. There was something else Akar wanted me to tell the man," I added.

"What was that?"

"Akar wanted me to explain why the fire happened."

"You mean there was a reason?"

106

"I asked the man if he knew why it happened and he said he wasn't sure. So, I explained Spirit told me it had something to do with the fire purification ceremony they do at Ananda every Sunday before service. The people that weren't supposed to be at Ananda Village when it was first getting started were supposed to leave. The man mentioned there had been some dissension and that is exactly what happened, some left," I concluded.

"That is pretty amazing, Jan," said Lucia. "Look, there is our turn off. We are here."

"Lucia, you have no idea how much today means to me. I wanted to know how to find the metaphysical stores in Auburn but couldn't, and then you took me to them. I've wanted a Zen Garden for a few years now, and then I saw one."

"I didn't think you were going to get the Zen Garden," said Lucia with a surprised look on her face.

"It's being worked out. That is all I know," I laughed.

"Girl, you are strange, but I love you," she laughed, parking the car.

"Now we are here going to the Altar Show. There will be energy from dead bodies, ghosts, witches ...."

"Slow down, Jan. I didn't say anything about dead bodies and ghosts or witches. We were talking about energy and wanting to check out the altars," reminded Lucia.

"Well, I can't wait to see what we are in store for," I said with a big smile, stepping out of the car.

Chapter 10

"Lucia, look at all the people coming and going through the open gate to the fairgrounds. The altar show is free," I rejoiced.

"They didn't charge the last time I went either." Lucia commented as she pulled the sleeves of her sweat jacket over her arms.

I grabbed my blue jacket and put it on. It was barely raining but the sight of the tall pine trees surrounding the fairgrounds in the icy cold weather made one feel like it was going to snow any minute.

We walked down an asphalt pathway leading to a red building that had a huge white banner on it with the letters, Altar Show, written on it in dark blue with an emblem in the left-hand corner that I couldn't make out. Dark green shrubs in different sizes were growing beneath it.

I glanced at the empty wooden concession stand to the right of us, and for a split second, I could see people gathered around it, talking to each other while they put mustard on hot dogs, and children ate cotton candy. Sounds of screams and laughter echoed from the Ferris wheel packed with riders as it went round and round over an area where it once stood that was now barren dirt.

"It's hard to believe we are here, Lucia. I never dreamed I would be going to an altar show today. I am sure glad we canceled our original plans of going to an art show in Sacramento."

"We will still be seeing art on display, but this creative art will have energy attached to it that is very different," Lucia responded.

"Yeah, ghosts, goblins, and …."

"There you go again," Lucia laughed as if pleased with my enthusiasm.

We opened the door and walked into an enormous room where a woman greeted us and handed each of us a yellow program that explained what we would be seeing.

"Is this your first time at the Altar Show?" she asked.

"Yes! It's my first time," I spoke up.

"Wonderful," her eyes beamed.

"I have been here before," said Lucia taking the program from the woman's extended hand.

"Enjoy yourselves."

I was drawn to a silk salmon-colored tent trimmed in gold. The point at the top made the tent look like a sultan's tent. A black stuffed monkey with a funny red hat was looking right at us. It was sitting on a tall skinny beige chest with five drawers on it that looked somewhat out of place. A life-sized ape sat on top of the tent with its legs hanging over the draped open front door.

"It's okay to go in, Jan. This is a hands-on exhibit," explained Lucia nodding her head affirmatively.

I pulled back the drape and entered, expecting to find a harem of women on the inside, all of whom would be feeding their masters grapes. Instead, when I stepped into the room, I found my eyes scanning a two-leveled display. There was so much to take in.

"Go ahead and sit on the wooden bench, Jan. That is why it is here," coaxed Lucia.

"Thanks," I sat down, facing the display and didn't say a word as my eyes studied it. Two crisscrossed paint brushes with mixed colors of paint on their handles pointed to a plain white card with letters printed on it, "YOU HAVE MY WHOLE HEART FOR MY WHOLE LIFE." This item appeared on the upper level. Behind the brushes I saw a circus car with miniature apes, wild cats, and other animals peering out the windows. The large head of a court jester looked at you from the left hand corner. Four inch skeletons dangled on each side of the display.

On the bottom level, a stack of photos caught my eye. They looked like family members. An elderly couple was sitting at a dinner table posing for the camera. The gray-haired woman and the man next to her were both nicely dressed for the special occasion they must have been celebrating. A young woman was holding a child on her right hip, and in another photo a man was standing on a boat on a lake showing off the big fish he caught. Miniature pieces were scattered throughout the display, one resembling a scary ghost.

A man entered the tent, so I got up.

"Excuse me," I said, exiting the tent.

Lucia was patiently waiting for me on the outside.

"The displays actually start over there," she said, pointing across the room.

"Someone really put a lot of creative effort inside the tent of this display," I commented as we walked back over to the entrance.

"You can feel it. Even the tent itself took a lot of thought and work," remarked Lucia.

The first display of the show was called "An Altar to My Altars." The woman had been making altars for the altar show since 1999, according to the program. At first, she didn't consider herself an artist until someone pointed out to her that she really was one. Now, she was claiming that she was, and the photos displayed all the creative altars she had made.

Some of the displays at the altar show were dedicated to causes such as to all domestic violence victims, ones who survived and those who didn't. Another one was showing how the people in Palestine had been uprooted by Israel and how U.S. tax dollars were involved. There was also a life-sized male mannequin dressed in red-white-and-blue that resembled Uncle Sam wearing a tall striped hat. A sign above it read, "Emergency Room," and the sign below attached to the table read, "Peace is the Cure."

Before we left the first room to enter the second, Lucia and I both sat down on a bench facing a peaceful scene. Large cut limbs, some two feet high, others a little taller, sat on the concrete floor framing a small peaceful stage with the picture of a couple posing in front of a lake. Chunks of moss draped cut limbs. Lit candles flickered in small glass votive candle holders. Religious statues were sitting on tall homemade pillars of different heights. Two statues I had never seen before were of Kuan Yin, who was holding a baby, and the other one was a small statute of a bearded Christ sitting in a Buddhist meditation position. His hands were in front of him with thumbs touching index-fingers, a position known as a Mudra (symbolic hand gesture) that I recognized.

The second room we entered was also fascinating. Most of the displays had pictures of the person the altar was created to honor. For example, one had a large picture of a young cowboy. Near the picture sat his hat, boots, and other possessions that once belonged to him. But the altar display that really caught my attention wasn't elaborate at all. It was a simple one.

"Lucia, look at this. The energy coming from this altar display is very powerful," I called out, with my eyes studying the small table with a black lace shawl covering it. Sitting on the table were two pictures and a crystal ball with Tarot cards spread next to it. Behind the display was a handmade quilt with one inch squares on it in different colors with a bright orange symbol in the middle that resembled two crescent moons facing opposite directions with a full moon or sun in the middle.

"The skull with the tiny flashing colored lights, a pentagram, and two tall candles are pretty creepy," said Lucia, pointing under the table.

A chill came over my body as I heard the voice of a woman suddenly standing behind me, causing me to think she may have flown in rather than walked up to me.

I turned around to see jet black hair flowing down the face of a woman who may have been in her late twenties.

"Hi," she greeted us with an outstretched hand.

"Hello," I responded, cautiously reaching out my hand and touching hers for a faint hand shake that made me feel like she might be a mirage rather than a real person.

"Do you like the display?" she questioned me, studying my eyes as if perusing my very soul.

"I was pulled in by the powerful energy emanating from it," I said, turning to study it.

"This is my display. I created it," she boasted, perking up.

"The skull on the floor is an interesting touch," said Lucia smirking.

"My soul mate, the lighting god, made it," the woman beamed as she looked towards the young man approaching her who was within hearing distance.

My eyes exchanged a questionable glance with Lucia's.

"I am really happy you can feel the energy that went into creating the display. The quilt has my menstrual blood in it, my urine, and hair," she beamed as she looked up at it alongside of her lighting god side-kick who was also proudly gazing at it.

I was so shocked by what she said that I found myself putting up a wall to protect myself from her. So, I wasn't sure if she ever mentioned from what part of her body the hair came. She mentioned a psychic association with which she was associated. Though she didn't come out and say the word, I knew by the human ingredients she used in the quilt and the pentagram near it, that she was a witch, a real witch, the kind that live and breathe and walk around right by us and without our ever knowing they are witches.

"Do you set your quartz crystals outside during a storm to let the lightening charge them?" I asked, showing off. It was something I had been taught by a woman claiming to be a witch, who had once sold me some stones on Ebay. I actually did it once, which was actually a lot of fun. I remember getting soaked and fearing I would get struck down by lightening as I spread several crystals over the wet lawn in back of my house.

"Of course I put the crystals out when there is lightening," she spoke up.

Lucia just looked down at everything on the display table and didn't say a word.

"The picture of the building in the background on the table has a ghost in front of it. And the woman in the picture is my mother who is deceased," she explained pointing with her index finger to the picture.

"That is a cool picture of the ghost," acknowledged Lucia.

"Thanks. I took it...."

Once again I felt myself putting up a kind of emotional wall of protection between myself and the woman, so I never heard where she said she snapped the picture.

'It was nice meeting you," I said as I started walking towards the next display. Lucia followed close behind me.

"Same, here, I am glad you liked the display," she said as she watched us turn a corner and disappear into another room.

"Witches, dead people, ghosts, we got it all in that display," I giggled as I looked around the dimly lit room we just entered. "I guess it turned out to be that kind of an altar show after all."

"You wanted ghosts, witches, and dead people," chided Lucia.

My favorite display was in the next room. A small structure had been built that had a room we also entered. Lovely pieces of carved wood were attached to the outside of the structure and were painted gold. It made me feel like I was looking at tall pipes from a chord organ or French horns, but it was just a bunch of stuff that kept giving off different impressions of what it represented. When I walked through the tight-fitting door, the scene I gazed upon was that of the Universe. Tiny lights twinkled on huge balls that may have been made of latex that were touching each other. The whole room had stars glimmering all around.

"I'm HOME," my soul cried out as loudly as a mental thought could. I was gazing upon my stars in an endless galaxy. It was an astrologer's dream come true.

We exited. Lucia and I walked passed a display that was made to honor thirteen Native American grandmothers who were gathered from the four directions to pray for peace. Another display honored babies born to women in prison that died at birth or were still-born. It represented a cemetery back East somewhere where smalls gray stones with a single letter of the alphabet on each one of them marked the graves.

When we exited the show, we noticed that it had been raining. We held our jackets tightly closed to keep warm as we raced towards the car.

"Thanks for bringing me here, Lucia," I beamed. "What a wonderful gift for celebrating my birthday.

"I am so glad you liked it, Jan," she replied.

"Wasn't that witch something else? I spoke up.

"What did you think about that handshake?" asked Lucia.

"I don't remember shaking her hand," I remarked.

"We both shook her hand. You can tell a lot about a person by their handshake," she commented.

"I don't understand."

"Her handshake was like a feather," she said.

"Oh."

"She didn't have much confidence," she explained.

"I suspect someone playing with the black arts lacks something," I laughed.

"You got that right," Lucia spoke up.

"I will drive back, Lucia. The altar show seems to have revived me," I said as I got back into the car.

"It's amazing how much energy you can pull from something like that," she commented.

"When I stood before the display of the cowboy, for a moment I could see him standing there wearing the hat and the shoes and looking back at me," I said as I drove down the road.

"I felt that way too when I stood before the thirteen Native American grandmothers. It was as if I could see them in the four directions, praying for peace. It was one of my favorite displays," said Lucia.

"I am still thinking about whether or not I should buy the Zen sand garden," I mumbled distantly.

"The Zen sand garden...? I thought you changed your mind about buying it," Lucia remarked with a surprised look in her eyes.

"It was just resting in my thoughts. I still haven't decided. Do you remember what time the lady said she would be closing at the Quiet Path store?"

"I think she said five-thirty."

"It's four now," I said glancing at the clock on the dash.

"We have enough time, but I am surprised that you would want to buy it when you can make it so much cheaper. We even found a nice tray for it at the thrift store when we were there," reminded Lucia.

"You know me, Lucia. I am a bargain hunter and often take broken things and fix them back up like new. But this time it is different. This feeling has to do with direction I am getting from Akar."

"What does your Spirit guide have to do with buying a Zen sand garden?"

"It has to do with something I experienced in a conversation with GOD one time," I quipped.

"God? How did God get into it? That is a pretty big leap to go from Spirit guide to God," Lucia remarked.

"I believe they are both the same thing," I reasoned.

"What conversation did you have with God?"

"It happened when I first moved back to California from Missouri. A Unity Minister who was a friend of mine was going to have a workshop at a church I had been attending. I made him his favorite chocolate chip with coconut cookies that I knew he liked. The move was costly, and money was a bit scarce. I couldn't decide if I should pay $35, which was the cost of the workshop, or if I should just stay home. My friend, the minister, would still get the basket of cookies. I knew he would be surprised to see me because he didn't know I had moved back in California," I said.

"What did you decide to do?"

"I was standing in the deep water at the corner of the swimming pool in the apartment of where I was living. The morning sun was warm, and I was very relaxed as I looked at the blue sky with only three small clouds in it. 'Go to the workshop,' said God. 'Why should I spend what little money I have to hear something I pretty much already know?' I asked." I explained to my friend.

"Let me see if I got this right. You questioned, GOD?" asked Lucia with a look of shock on her face.

"Yep. I knew it was God. He said, 'Go to the workshop. Your friend needs the money because money has also been scarce for him. People pray for me to help them all the time, but

I can't drop a new automobile down from heaven or arrive at someone's front door with a wad of money. It doesn't work that way,' God explained to me," I replied.

"So, how does it work?" asked Lucia. "How did God say it works when people pray for something they need or want?"

"According to him, it is people on Earth getting inspired to help someone and then acting on it that serves him. They are the ones that do what he can't physically do because He cannot force us against our will. Then he inspires someone to help them in return," I answered.

"I get what you are saying on how prayers get answered, but what does it have to do with the Zen sand garden?" quizzed Lucia.

"I am being drawn to buy what may end up being Simba's sandbox," I laughed. "Could you try calling her on your cell phone and see if the store will be open?"

"Sure." Lucia reached into her purse to get her cell phone. "I keep getting a busy signal," she said frowning a few minutes later.

"Good. At least that means she is still there."

When we arrived at the Quiet Path, the woman I talked to earlier was getting ready to close for the day.

"I came back to buy the Zen garden," I smiled, walking over to view it again. Nothing had been tampered with. There were still five gray slate rocks, some lying down and others standing up. A mud man sat on a crystal slab, and a small starfish was in the white sand. A small crystal ball was mounted on a small stand buried in the sand. Tiny fake metal green trees were in it.

"The box is missing. I am not sure how to wrap it up for you," the tired frail old woman said, sorting through bags until she found a really big one.

"Can I pay you for it now?" I asked.

"The cash register isn't working," she muttered confused.

I thought that was strange, but could see she was feeling overwhelmed with the transaction, so I waited to pay her.

The black pottery base fit in the large bag with the sand and small items were packaged in a smaller one. The sign read, "Cash only," so I counted out all the cash I had in my purse, which was exactly the right amount.

"How has business been for you in this store," I asked, trying to get confirmation that my transaction was helping her.

"It's been really bad for the past couple of years," she answered with a weary look on her face.

"Christmas is coming, so it might pick up now."

"I hope so," she smiled.

Lucia and I were exhausted when we finally got to my home. I fixed her a hot cup of Mexican chicken and tortilla soup along with some crackers and garlic roasted humus that had roasted pine nuts in it.

"Thanks so much for this meal, Jan. It tastes marvelous ... especially since it is so cold outside."

"I am glad you like it," I beamed.

That night, shortly after Lucia left, I spent hours carefully setting up my Zen garden. In my office, I have a maple cabinet with class doors that proudly display three shelves of stones from all over the world. At first, I put turquoise stones in the Zen garden, but I pulled them out and put just plain quartz crystals with a small white selenite Buddha. There were about a million different layouts I could do. My inner child was having a ball. I finally decided on four flagstone rocks, one large apophyllite crystal and the tiny mud man. Apophyllite was made up of tiny crystals and is considered a journeying stone when one wanted to venture into other dimensions. Next, I took the small bamboo rake and ran it across the sand.

I stood, admiring my creation, happy that I had decided to buy it. Just then, Simba walked into the room. I had forgotten about Simba and my reservations about getting the garden for years.

Later, when I went to bed I lay awake thinking about my magical day with Lucia. One metaphysical store, a thrift store, the baby doll I found there for my granddaughter, and the altar show -- what better day could anyone ask to enjoy?

The next morning, when I awoke, I looked up to find Simba standing next to me with his eyes peering down at me. I could read his mind, "FOOD, NOW!"

I jumped up out of bed and ran to the living room, heading straight for the Zen garden. A smile came over my face. One of the rocks had been moved a tiny bit, and there were two marks that resembled paw prints, but none of the sand had been pawed out, and there were no other surprises that I had feared he would leave behind. My garden was safe for now.

Chapter 11

It was Sunday morning. I stood before my bathroom mirror, noticing all the new white hairs I had earned with age. I was fortunate because the white hairs contrasted with my dark ash-blonde hair, giving me the appearance of frosted hair that framed my face, which I should have had to pay a beautician a lot of money to create for me but was instead totally natural.

I had twenty minutes to get dressed and get to the Ananda Temple in time for the purification ceremony. Today, I chose black slacks with a purple tank top and a purple bat-sleeved cotton cardigan that hung down long enough to cover my hips. My shoes were black leather sandals with a one-inch heel on them that I could easily slip off. It wasn't mandatory that shoes had to be removed, but I never liked standing before the altar with shoes on my feet.

Everyone stood up when the two Nayaswamis entered the room, wearing beautiful blue garments that draped their bodies. Orange robes were the traditional color of garments worn by spiritual leaders in Ananda. However, in 2010 Swami Kriyananda created a new monastic order for the purpose of renouncing ego and earthly desires that distracted from the Swamis' commitments to God. Whenever I saw someone wearing a blue robe, I knew they fought a battle against physical desires much greater than the battles once fought by Roman soldiers.

The Swami leading the purification ceremony tossed ghee, a clarified butter, into the fire, which was flaming in a small metal bowl and sitting on a tall wooden stand just wide enough to hold the round silver tray on which the bowl sat. Tossing the

JANICE A. STORK

ghee into flames represented devotion of the heart and its power to transcend. Next, they tossed rice, representing our work and efforts, into the burning flames to connect us to the divine. Everyone partaking in the ceremony stood around the flames, repeating uplifting chants.

In my hand was a tiny strip of white paper. I glanced at it to make sure I didn't forget the words I would say when I knelt down before one of the seated Swamis. It said, "I seek purification by the Grace of God." The piece of paper was blank beneath the words, so I could write something in pencil that inwardly and privately I wanted to offer up to God. This prayer request could be a spiritual quality I wanted to enhance or an obstacle I wanted to remove out of my way. In some cases, the words written were those of thanks and gratitude for an issue that had been resolved from a previous prayer request.

After the Swami meditated with me silently for a moment, he said a few words and then touched my heart but never seeing what was written on my paper. Slowly, I walked before the altar, so that I could stand before a burning candle where I used its flame to light the paper before tossing it into a metal bowl. Next, I stood before the pictures of Christ and several Gurus (spiritual teachers) and spoke from my heart, often times feeling that the eyes I gazed upon were looking back at me.

Sometimes the requests that I placed in the burning bowl were for guidance in dealing with difficult heart-felt issues. During such times, songs the choir sung during the service would bring tears to my eyes. A perfect example was when I learned my son, Jon, aged 40, had been diagnosed with an inoperable brain tumor that the doctors felt could have been growing for 30 years. Though the experience was part of his journey in life, I found my heart breaking when I watched him walk down an unfamiliar path marked with dangerous radiation and chemo therapy treatments.

121

My son was loved by many friends. Before long, churches of every denomination were praying for him all over the world. Logically, I was grateful for the prayers and encouraging words he received from his support team, but I was a skeptic. When it came to prayers I felt God (Divine Mother, Christ, Saints of all religions, Great Spirit, Universe, Paramahansa Yogananda, Gurus, and any name of an unseen Divine Force) already knew whatever was being asked. I, however, revisited my thoughts on prayer when my son got word from his cancer specialists that the cancer had backed off, and the prognosis was that he would be around to enjoy life for many years to come. This amazing news was like a miracle, considering the fact that these same doctors had stated that the tumor was inoperable despite the fact that Jon did his part by jogging, eating wholesome foods, and giving up sugar.

Now, when I scribbled my words on my tiny white piece of paper, they were no longer related to the journey on which I followed my son, sometimes having to crawl along the long road that took almost a year to reach resolution. Now, the tiny strip of white paper, instead, had words written in pencil that said, "Help me not like cake! By the way, Lord, that word cake represents all the foods that constantly tempt me." Sometimes, I would glance at the picture of Swami Paramahansa Yogananda, who had a big belly hidden beneath his robe and laugh to myself, "I am not the only one who liked cake." Yogananda's eyes would twinkle as he smiled back at me.

I noticed something magical happened when I wrote those words on a tiny piece of paper, begging for help related to FOOD, then burned them, and offered them up to Spirit. The following week my son told me he was reading the book called the *Bhagavad Gita*. I had owned this two volume set of books many times in my life, but I found the writing to be over my head, so I would just give them to other people, thinking it might help them on their spiritual journey.

"Mom, it isn't that difficult to read," my son, Jon, said one day.

A week later, I noticed the Bhagavad Gita in the Ananda book store; it was a volume that had been interpreted by Paramahansa Yogananda. The writings had something to do with dialogue between two people and about a battle being fought.

"Why in the world would I want to read a book about a battle? I have always been against wars. Battles and confrontations of wills always turn me off," I reasoned to myself in my mind. But then there was the prevailing thought that followed, "If my son said he could read it, and thoroughly loved it, surely I could."

Suddenly, the prayer which I had carefully handprinted on the folded little piece of paper I held between my fingers that asked for help to not like cake was being answered. I sat in my patio next to a wrought-iron table with matching chairs. Towering above me were two California Redwoods, standing three or four stories high. I began reading and taking notes as fast as I could, so I would remember the who was who for each of the characters with the impossible to pronounce Indian names.

The Bhagavad Gita tells the story of a Blind King that represents our minds; therefore, the king is called the Blind Mind. Our body is the chariot and the soul is the owner of the chariot. Horses pulling the chariot represent our senses we send to the blind mind that sends the messages back down the reins, directing the horses where to take us. The King has children. The Pandu children are pure at heart and the good kids. The Kurus are the wicked children who feed off the senses and mental impulses.

Eating cake was not what was eating me. What was eating me was that I felt I had spent my whole life, studying the works of great masters, learning to be centered, and helping people in my astrology practice which sometimes included messages from my guide, Akar, yet I wasn't strong enough to overcome a ravishing desire to eat everything in sight. My belief that I was weak was what was eating me.

From the Bhagavad Gita I learned the battle was a battle that every man does with himself every day of his life. The book mentions an Indian word, samskaras, which means habits to which we fall victim and reinforce each time we do the habit again.

Suddenly, it became clear that I was responding to impulses around me, but I also discovered that I did have control. Within a few days, I lost a couple of pounds. A few weeks later, I lost another ten pounds, and after a few short months, I had lost over twenty pounds. My battle was over, and food was no longer a threat. I never felt like I was punishing myself for not having something because if I wanted it I had it. It was then that I also learned something I heard that helped me a lot. It was that white flour and white sugar can cause a lot of cravings, so I went through my cupboards and threw them all out. But I still had to be careful. It was easy to forget to be mindful when my day was too busy; the old habits would lurk and sometimes the Kurus, those bad children, won. The next morning I would step on the scale and see I gained back a pound or two; thus, I would try to bring myself back to center again, knowing I was in control of the little brats who spent so much time teasing and tempting me. And those little brats were nothing more than my senses having a field day.

The next time when I wrote something on the strip of paper that I tossed into the burning bowl, it simply read, "Thank you."

Paramahansa Yogananda's eyes twinkled, and his smile touched my heart as I turned to look into Christ's eyes.

"All you had to do is ask," Christ reminded me when our eyes met.

The feeling of gratitude stayed with me as I sat in my seat, waiting for the morning service which began 15 minutes after the purification ceremony.

I often experienced many profound insights that involved other dimensions during morning services. Once during the service, I had a vision of three spiritual leaders that popped into my mind during meditation at different times throughout that service. What surprised me is that their spiritual teachings were so different from each other, and two of them I wouldn't find in an Ananda Temple. The first person I saw was Swami Kriyananda, the founder of Ananda. I didn't think it was too unusual to see him there because he had visited the Temple in Sacramento many times in the past, so his vibration would still be there. However, that particular day when the Nayaswami got up to give his morning message, his talk was about Swami Kriyananda. He recalled working with him and shared things the Swami had said to him when he first came to Ananda Village in Nevada City. I assumed I saw him in the Temple because I was picking up the thoughts of the Nayaswami about to talk about him.

A little while later, during the same service, with my eyes closed, I had a vision of the Buddhist Dalai Lama, but before the service concluded the Catholic Pope also appeared. I understood Swami Kriyananda being in the Temple, but why in the world would the Dalai Lama and the Pope appear before me during the same service?

Akar explained to me that during meditation we can put ourselves into a different vibration where the brain waves actually change. What I was doing was like fine tuning a radio station to a place or station where we connect with a higher consciousness

(God, Divine Mother, Christ, Saints of all religions, Great Spirit, Universe, Paramahansa Yogananda, Gurus, and any name of an unseen Divine Force).

On that particular day, it was like I went to a water troth in prayer where Swami Kriyananda, the Dalai Lama, and the Pope were drinking from the same water or in prayer at the same time; therefore, I saw them. In that place where we all met, we were all the same. It didn't matter what road to God we took, the design or the color our clothes, or what race we were. We met through a vibration where we were all the same.

Suddenly, it all made sense. Every time I had visions or heard things from a fourth dimension, I was accessing it during quiet moments when I, Jan, got out of my own way. Often times, music was the vibration that took me to that other realm.

I also recalled the time I had a really hectic day and was exhausted. I curled up on my sofa that sat beneath my picture window in my living room and looked out at the birch tree that was swaying in the wind. It was one of those times when I didn't say I heard Akar. Instead, it was God Himself who was talking to me.

"Look at the tree. The wind is moving its branches, and its body bends, while it is swaying to and fro," God said.

It was so peaceful to have my body at rest and to watch the tiny leaves that were glistening in the sun.

"The birch isn't distracted by the garage sale across the street or all the cars coming and going. However, like you, the tree has its battles, too. It fights off the Sacramento heat where temperatures get up to 108 degrees in the summer; and the freezing cold in the winter when temperatures can fall below 20 degrees. But it still stands, centered only on what it is doing."

"God, why have you waited so long to talk to me?" I asked.

"You haven't sat still in a long time," He answered, causing me to smile.

My thoughts wandered back to the Temple where I had sat in the pew and looked around the room. Christ's picture was on the wall in front of me, accompanied by the pictures of several gurus cascading down from it. Below all of the pictures was a beautiful altar adorned with fresh picked flowers and a golden silk cloth that swirled around flickering candles.

I shook my head as I thought some Christians would think it was wrong to sit in a temple with pictures of other great spiritual leaders on the wall besides just Christ. Woven into that thought was my realization that the judgments from different religious denominations that claimed their path was the right one had caused a lot of chaos in the world. This realization troubled me deeply. I wanted to shout, "It is all the same. Great Divine Force In Sky – GOD - many paths lead to Him. People can't see the error in their judgments -- only the duality that often times led to wars.

I looked around the room. People were still taking their seats. The pews were almost full, and service would be starting any minute.

I thought about the year 2012 in which we were presently living. Many prophets and psychics had foretold that this year would be a time of gloom and doom, particularly because the Mayan Calendar would be coming to an end. As an astrologer, I knew differently. I had done numerous astrology charts and could see changes coming but not the changes everyone feared.

Gloom and doom for the world was already happening now and had been for some time. Yet, people waited for the big thing they thought was going to happen. I had watched difficult planetary aspects between Saturn and Pluto that went back as far as the 9/11 incident in 2001 when terrorists attacked the United States and killed thousands of our people with their hijacked planes that struck the Twin Towers in New York. It took seven years for Saturn to square Pluto again (2008) and when it did, Uranus was added to the mix, and the financial crisis occurred.

It wasn't just my calculations that revealed to me what was going to happen in the world. I remember when I woke up at 2:00 in the morning to Akar, who was explaining the cosmos to me and what the planetary aspects meant.

He said, "Saturn, the planet that has the nature of 'old father time' and the old ways of doing things, was in bad aspect to Pluto. Pluto has the nature of youth, destroying in order to rebuild, and new ways of doing things. No one wanted to budge until Uranus came into aspect with these two planets. Uranus has the nature of unexpected destruction. Uranus forced things to get done through chaos and unexpected accidents or disasters."

What a gift Akar gave me. I never before attempted to ask him what impact the vibrations of the planets were having on the world. Yet, major events were happening exactly as he explained. Youth or new ways was the cry of people, all of whom were willing to risk their lives to bring down dictators and their old ways of ruling in the Middle East. Health care policies in the U.S. needed to be changed with old ways fighting the new. People marched on Wall Street, demanding a new way of dealing with money. Japan's nuclear power plant threatened the health of people in the world when its nuclear power plant was damaged by a massive earthquake. An oil rig exploding off shore in the United States caused us to have to look at new ways to drill for oil.

Everyone in the Temple stood up when the two Nayaswami's walked back into the room. The second service was about to begin.

The time flew by while they spoke, and the choir sang. My mind was still wrapped around what was happening in the world. It was a mess, and people waited for it to get worse, yet I knew the end of 2012 would usher in a new consciousness and difficult times would start letting up. I just didn't know what would trigger the change.

I looked up to see the service was starting to wrap up with the Festival of Light. This time was my favorite part of the service. Both Nayaswami's faced each other, looking up towards the flame of the candle. It was then that they told a story of a little bird's journey, which represented a person's path towards self-realization, which wasn't always easy.

Once again, my mind thought, "How sad. What would happen if you took such a beautiful ceremony and put it in the middle of a corn field where people gathered, and the Nayaswami's wore the same robes with both gazing up to the candle one was holding? Most likely, there would be angry people who would say that these innocent holy spiritual leaders were practicing witchcraft or belonged to a cult, and try to hurt them."

This thought quickly took me to the thought I often had where I wondered what Christians would do if they saw Christ, wearing a long beard and sandals, walking down the street today. "They would shun him as a homeless beggar," I suspected.

The service concluded with people walking up to the Nayaswami's to be blessed.

The services at Ananda were deeply inspiring for me. I always walked away feeling refreshed from words I heard spoken. My favorite quote from Swami Paramahansa Yogananda was, "Circumstances are always neutral. It is our reaction to them that gives them meaning for us and making them appear either good or bad, pleasant or unpleasant."

However, today I didn't walk away feeling at peace at all. I was hungry for more answers about the plight of the world and how it could get bailed out. Little did I know I was about to get them.

Chapter 12

The hands on the clock pointed to midnight. I had been tossing and turning for a couple of hours unable to go to sleep. Each evening before I go to sleep I review my day. If there is anything upsetting to me, I imagine a big fire, and then I toss what is upsetting me into the flames. It was something I learned from Ananda. This time, it didn't seem to work. Perhaps it didn't work because what was bothering me didn't just relate to me.

For a moment, I remembered a birthday card some students gave to me when I was a teenager. It had a cartoon picture on it of someone humped over and carrying the weight of the world on his shoulders. My friends were teasing me for taking life so seriously, while they laughed and had fun. It seemed surreal to think that I was still the same person, worrying about what was going on in the world despite all I had learned about life since then.

The more I thought about what was going on throughout the world, the more I got upset. Now, I couldn't go to sleep and feared I might never sleep again. There didn't seem to be a solution to all the chaos, and it was frightening.

"Earth will never be destroyed as long as it serves as a school for souls incarnating into bodies to have a human experience," said Akar, sensing fear coming from me.

"Earth is not the only thing I am concerned about," I said softly.

"You mean drip? That idea is what you are thinking," he responded.

"Dearest Akar. Only you could have known about the drips in my mind. Before I went to bed tonight, I tuned into a couple of the major news stations on television that people throughout the world were watching. Drip was the story of nuclear weapons being manufactured in Iran -- a country that is angry and hungry for power. The story wasn't scary enough, so the media reporting it added the words, 'growing fears that an atomic bomb could be coming out of Iran.' Drip, Drip was the economic crisis that left millions of people out of jobs. Drip, Drip, Drip was the story on global warming," I conveyed from my mind.

"My student has learned well. You are looking at life from another dimension -- unattached -- and you are seeing the big picture. I see it in your thoughts that are swelling," Akar pointed out.

"The threat isn't the story being reported in the news. The story itself is the drip, and it is much the same as Chinese water torture, but it isn't water .... It is fuel. Each story is a drop of negativity, spreading across one land ... one and then another. The stories don't stop. When they are broadcast, they have a dark heavy vibration, causing them to block out the sun. And the sun is our serenity and peace of mind. The news media is feeding off power fed by ratings. Now networks have caught on to social media. So, they ask that viewers go to Twitter and tweet them or go to Facebook and send them their thoughts on what is being reported. Millions of people are doing just that. Oh!.... My gosh!" I gasped to myself.

"Their monitors and modems are becoming gods," said Akar.

"Yes. You are still reading my mind. People hear a ding and suddenly become disengaged from whomever they are with when they look down at their iPhones to see who has texted them. These technological devices have people emailing strangers they don't even know or playing games with opponents that don't even exist. In the meantime, they are no longer communicating with their spouse or children. Sometimes, they are not even doing their jobs that they are being paid to do while they are being distracted by these electronic devices. It is all false," I cried out with no one to warn.

"You are seeing the truth of what is happening about which most people are not even aware, but you have wandered to a place that has you upset," said Akar.

"Something isn't right, Akar. I have calculated numerous astrology charts for the end of this year, 2012, and it is supposed to begin a time when peoples' consciousnesses change to something more positive. However, I can see an event locked into this summer that looks upsetting on a large scale, perhaps global, but it is short-lived. People will be frightened, but it is just a bump in the road that causes a big jolt. After that time, the major planets, which were causing havoc for years, make favorable aspects; pressures let up, and there is hope again. A positive consciousness will prevail. I am aware that the presidential election is at the end of the year, but I don't know if that has something to do with it or not."

I was well aware of the important role bumps played in people's lives. I was quiet for a moment as I reached inside my mind to memories that stood out relating to bumps that got people back on track. In one incident, I recalled there was a woman who was extremely upset with her boyfriend, who just happened to be a high-ranking legislator where we both worked. He was seeing someone else and lying to her about it. It made her so upset that the anger was consuming her. A couple of days later, she bumped her leg on one of the desks in the Senate chambers, and it became severely swollen. I saw her right after that day when I stopped by her office to say hello. When I went into the office and spoke to her for a few minutes, I could see that she wasn't worried about her boyfriend anymore, despite the fact that he had made her feel so angry at one time. Now, all she talked about was her black and blue leg. The dark energy had to be released, and running into the desk was the bump that jarred it out of her.

I also recalled another incident when I was sitting in a hot tub when I lived in a condo. A man was helping his male friend get into the hot, bubbling water. Something was wrong with his friend's leg. When I asked the friend about it, he said a car hit and run him. I told him I was an astrologer and asked if I could have his birth date, so I could see if something was showing up in his chart that related to the accident. His chart had to be calculated in my mind, but I did see something pop out from the crude calculations.

I said, "You were really angry about something involving a loved one that you thought betrayed you."

Of course, the strange thing about betrayal shown by Neptune in a chart is that I can never tell who is doing the betraying. Then he told me how accurate I was because he had been upset with his wife who asked him for a divorce. He was furious about it. The part that seemed odd is that he was gay, and he was with his gay lover in the hot tub. His wife just wanted to move on with her life. I explained that the driver in the car was doing him a favor. The built-up negative energy was consuming him, and it had to be released. He got it. He understood. And he wasn't angry with his wife anymore. The bump of the accident shifted his consciousness, so he could calm down enough in his mind to be able to see where she was coming from. Now, his thoughts turned to his leg and the stupid driver that caused the hit and run accident. I just got out of the hot tub without sharing that the driver may have been his angel.

I could feel Akar's presence as he watched my mind trying desperately to take the incidences I was remembering and tie them into the ugly state of affairs going on in the world. Then I realized that Mother Earth was doing the same thing to protect itself from the dark energy circling the planet. There were earthquakes, flash floods, fires, tornados, and hurricanes happening all over the world that were trying to bump off the negative energy being created by people's thoughts and actions. It was then that I suddenly understood that people were acting the way they were because they were frightened. Somehow, the new aspects the planets would make at the end of the year would set the stage for an event, or new laws that would turn things around, so people would no longer be as guarded as they were now. Once they let their guards down, they could see the positive things that were happening around them that they couldn't see now.

That realization was the one certain thing I had learned about life and honored. It was like a rule or truth for me: "So on the inside ... so on the outside." What was happening around me on the outside world mirrored what was going on inside me. The same rule was true for the world.

My mind raced, scanning thought after thought.

"Everything is talking to us all the time. All we have to do is look and listen to hear what Spirit wants to convey to us," I reasoned.

"That statement is true," Akar calmly acknowledged as he read my mind. "Remember the fire you saw at Ananda Village? It happened back in 1976, yet you saw it 35 years later even though you never knew there had been a fire. Its energy was still there, or you wouldn't have seen it. When an angry person takes a gun or knife and kills someone, the victim dies, but the dark negative energy still lives on. The 9/11 incident, which was perpetrated by terrorists, caused many people to die when their airplane struck the Twin Towers in New York. The passengers' bodies were removed prior to impact -- much the same way as what you said under hypnosis during that past life regression at your friend Dorothy's house. You saw your soul split off before the plane in which you flew crashed into the rock mountain and exploded. You didn't feel pain because your body crashed and was destroyed, but your soul lived on and was removed before the impact," he went on to explain.

I thought hard about what Akar was saying.

"When the terrorists attacked the United States, the President retaliated by going to war, adding more anger to the anger already created by the terrorists," he continued. When one of your soldiers died at war, his soul went home, ALIVE, back to GOD, where he came from before he was born on earth. Though gone in spirit, this person could see the loved ones left behind and at times those left behind could feel their loved one's presence that they lost, even if they couldn't explain it," he added.

I thought about what Akar said and had plenty of my own realizations, but I was more interested in his explanations. "Most of the time, when the person died, people left behind, such as parents, a spouse, children, siblings, lovers, and friends, were heartbroken and even angry. On the other side of the world, the same thing happened. When a soldier was killed, his soul went on but the energy from anger, pain and sorrow, survived. Not one, but thousands of soldiers died during the wars from both sides that were fighting. And the number of people who felt these emotions, from the loss of a loved one, were in the millions, and the energy of those emotions still lives," explained Akar.

"Wow. Added to those numbers were the people angry who didn't lose anyone. They were the ones who wanted to go to war. Then there were all the people who wanted peace. Their protests for peace came from angry hearts. Anger fueled anger. Now, the drip, drip, drip is like dropping kerosene on blazing fires," I said.

I was silent for a moment, but couldn't hold back totally and asked Akar the one question that I had to ask. "Everyone thinks there is a side that is right or wrong in all scenarios involving anger and a conflict. The parties involved even pray to God, as they know Him, hoping He will protect them. Who is the judge that decides which side of the conflict is right? Surely, the winner of a war is not the one that is right?"

"Jan. There is no one judging who is right or wrong. All that is happening is that a soul is experiencing what it is like to be human. There is no difference between being filthy rich or dirt poor. Nor is there any difference between being deathly sick or vibrantly healthy. The soul is having a human experience."

"But, Akar, if I do something really bad to someone, it seems to come back and kick me on my behind," I reasoned.

"Well, there is karma, which is simply a reaction to any action. It can be good or bad. One has to experience both sides of the coin. That's the law of the Universe you are seeing when something negative that you did or said to someone else comes back to haunt you in either a positive or a negative way. For some people, they won't even know what they did to incur the reaction, but trust me, they will face what they did -- if not in this lifetime, then in the next incarnation."

There was silence. Then I heard Akar say, "You've just traveled through a portal to another dimension where you were able to look back at life on earth and see the big picture."

"It looks so different from where I stood. People don't see what they do on earth. Their acts and deeds are alive," I said as I grew quiet, while I absorbed in my mind all that I was suddenly learning.

"It's okay, Jan. I see the thought you are debating and about to birth. Create it, and let it live," said Akar firmly.

"There is hope in all of this stuff, Akar. I saw a glimpse of it in the news," I said, amazed that light could shine through the negative stories being broadcast by television stations hungry for better ratings to secure their survival.

"Good for you," I heard Akar say. "The thought you are developing now is extremely important. Let it form. Let it out. Let it live. These thoughts are the key to the lives people live. Some people will never give birth to their thoughts that start to form or pay attention to what their spirit guides are trying to tell them in their minds. You are not any different than anyone else, Jan. You just knew you were in school."

"Gabby Giffords holds the key...." I started to blurt out the thought I had been pondering.

"Before you share your new insight, Jan, I must add something to what you are about to say. Your friend, Michael Bayard, gives up part of his life to share it with others. Many people gather for his drumming circles to listen to his extraordinary music. Michael has been journeying into other dimensions and working with higher beings to help heal Mother Earth and her inhabitants for some time. Your friend, Peter Clerin, in Canada, also creates music given to him from divine beings from other realms. He has seen these beings and astral traveled to other planets. His music profoundly affects those who hear it, much the same as Michael's music, while he helps to heal this planet. Both Peter's and Michael's music were brought into your life, so the divine vibration of their music could contribute to your seeing and hearing things in the fourth dimension. They fine-tuned you for me."

"I forgot about all the people who guided me in my lifetime, to where I am now, Akar," I replied.

138

"Finish what you wanted to say about Gabby," he instructed. "It is the key."

"Love, love, love. It is the hope and the light that can change the darkness circling this planet. Everyone close to death gets it, but no matter how many times they described it, those listening don't experience it. I did. I felt it in my near-death experience when the truck hit me. It was a love and warmth that fed my soul and took away every fear, causing me to want to die and go to the light, but it wouldn't let me because it wasn't time. The love was unconditional," I replied.

I paused for a moment and then continued, "Though I felt it at the time of the car accident, I have seen it since. I saw it in my son eyes when I watched Jon walk his journey after being diagnosed with a life-threatening cancerous brain tumor. His tears broke my heart. I felt helpless because I couldn't make it better. A mother wants to help her child even if he is a grown man. I wanted to use the one gift I was good at, astrology, to find answers. But instead, it had me confront my own fears when threatening bad aspects resulted in chemo therapy or radiation rather than his death, which I feared."

I could almost see Akar nod in agreement as I kept reflecting on what I had learned.

"Each time I died, but he lived, and his tears brought on by the thought of leaving behind his two beautiful children, children so young they hadn't even started school yet, cracked his heart open. I saw in his eyes and heard in his words the insights divine beings were sharing with him, words that kept him at peace and filled his heart full of love for everyone. It was the same divine love I felt in my near-death experience when the truck crashed in my car many years ago. I am sure his feelings of love were tweaked -- like when we apply a shock treatment to a heart that has stopped -- by all the countless prayers being said on his behalf. The prayers coming from people's hearts -- combined with the love rising from his own heart for others -- no doubt played an instrumental role in putting his life-threatening brain tumor in remission. It bought him many more years to spend enjoying his children and teaching them things from what he had learned," I finished.

Akar simply said, "Precisely," and I felt him move away, leaving me to my own thoughts.

I continued to reflect on all of the amazing things I had learned. It was in that moment that I realized three interesting things happened related to these two grandchildren and my journeying to the fourth dimension. My son and his wife weren't sure if they wanted to have children or not. One day, when I was driving away from their ranch house, I saw a little blonde girl playing where sheep once grazed, and knew I was seeing my future granddaughter. A year later, she was born, and today she looks just like the vision I had. Later, when a second child was being debated by my son and his wife, I had another vision. I was walking down the hall one day when I was visiting them in their home. I saw the family picture of my son and his wife with my granddaughter sitting on her mother's lap. This time, I saw a little boy sitting on my son's lap. About a year later, he was born.

A third amazing thing happened one night after midnight, while I sat thinking about my grandson. I was tired after babysitting my lively little granddaughter all day. Her mom and dad (my son) waited patiently in a delivery room for the birth of their baby. My heart was full of love for this little boy that we would soon get to meet. I sat at their kitchen counter and studied where the planets were in the sky that night. Akar started showing me a vision of my grandson's life, which included the work he would be doing -- flights in space -- and whether or not he would be married. I reached for several pieces of paper from a printer close by and maintained my relaxed

"Now you have graduated. You can go now and spend your final days really living," said Akar with his words touching my heart.

"Thank you," my heart sang out in my head. "Thank you, God, goddess, and all divine forces."

But for a moment, the gratitude that had welled up inside me slipped a bit. "Akar! Akar!" I shouted in panic.

"What is it?" he answered immediately.

"You are not going to leave me now, are you?"

"Since you asked that question, you've now been enrolled in summer school!" Akar said firmly.

"But I thought I knew all I needed to know."

"Apparently, NOT!"

"What don't I know?" I asked anxiously, waiting for his last words for now.

"You don't know who you are!"

"Ruff, Ruff," barked Max, "Ruff, Ruff, Ruff.

Suddenly, I heard the pet door flap open. Then, I saw Simba running, as fast as a fat cat can run, past my office. He was in hot pursuit of Max. Simba knew, if Max barked, something was wrong.

Once again, I could hear the pet door swing open and crash back down as my black cat, Kiera, raced passed my office. Kiera was not a first responder like Simba when Max barked. Most of the time, she ignored Max's warning.

"Ruff, Ruff," barked Max again.

I got up from the desk where I had been sitting and walked to my living room to see what was causing the commotion.

Both cats sat upright, watching Max bark at the water fountain sitting at the end table next to my black leather sofa. Water flowed through bamboo and made a loud trickling sound that echoed throughout the house.

"What is it, Max?" I questioned with a puzzled look on my face. Then, I turned away from him long enough to notice the back screen door to the patio was open.

"Ruff, Ruff," barked Max excitedly.

I stepped closer towards the fountain.

"No! No! Max," I called out.

Circling around the water fountain was a big, beautiful dragonfly.

"It won't hurt you, Max," I reassured my fluffy white dog. "It's okay," I informed both cats.

"Dragonfly is one of the Native American animal totems. This totem represents altered states, magic, and seeing through illusions. Its medicine helps remove the veil of anything in our world that might be out of control, such as addictions to drugs, food, or alcohol. The dragonfly must have seen the water and came in from outside to check it out," I explained to my animal audience that had all their eyes turned towards me, studying my human babble.

Suddenly, the dragonfly flitted past me on his way out the patio door, causing my eyes to really see the enormous picture that hung on my living room wall called, The Deva, by Michael Parkes. In the picture, a dragonfly is communicating to a woman where she sits on a stone marble slab with a wild cat behind her and a stone image of the cat lying flat by her feet. There is also a stone image of the dragonfly she is talking to lying flat by her feet. It looks like where she is sitting might be the top of a temple and clouds surround her. Then, I remembered the dragonflies I hung in the children's room in my home when Liberty was born. Above her crib in her home was a dragonfly I had painted. Outside in my yard were solar dragonflies hovering around my fountain.

When he flitted past me and showed me the picture, he must have been letting me know he's been my animal totem all along.

Both cats playfully followed the dragonfly out the door.

"Let him be, my pets. He's off on another adventure."

CPSIA information can be obtained
at www.ICGtesting.com
Printed in the USA
BVHW03s0532110418
513067BV00001B/336/P